UPRISING

THE LIBERATION OF DADRA AND NAGAR HAVELI

NEELESH KULKARNI

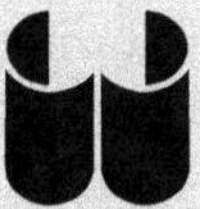

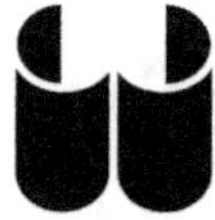

Published by Westland Non-Fiction, an imprint of Westland Books, a division of Nasadiya Technologies Private Limited, in 2024.

No. 269/2B, First Floor, 'Irai Arul', Vimalraj Street, Nethaji Nagar, Alapakkam Main Road, Maduravoyal, Chennai 600095

Westland, the Westland logo, Westland Non-Fiction and the Westland Non-Fiction logo are the trademarks of Nasadiya Technologies Private Limited, or its affiliates.

ISBN: 978-93-6045-865-2

10 9 8 7 6 5 4 3 2 1

Typeset by Mukul

Printed at Manipal Technologies Limited, Manipal

UPRISING

Neelesh Kulkarni is a management graduate, an entrepreneur, poet, theatre actor, voiceover artist, and a coach in public speaking and creative writing. He has also been a cricket commentator.

He is the author of the non-fiction work, *In the Footsteps of Rama* (HarperCollins India) which has been adapted into a web series and has been translated into two languages so far, with four more in progress. His essay, 'Vithoba of Pandharpur' has been anthologised in *Where the Gods Dwell: Thirteen Temples and their (hi)stories* (Westland). He has also written a book for children, *Open Sesame: Magic Tricks for Kids* (Westland).

He lives in Delhi with his artist wife.

For Sarita,
who wanted to see this book in print even more than I did

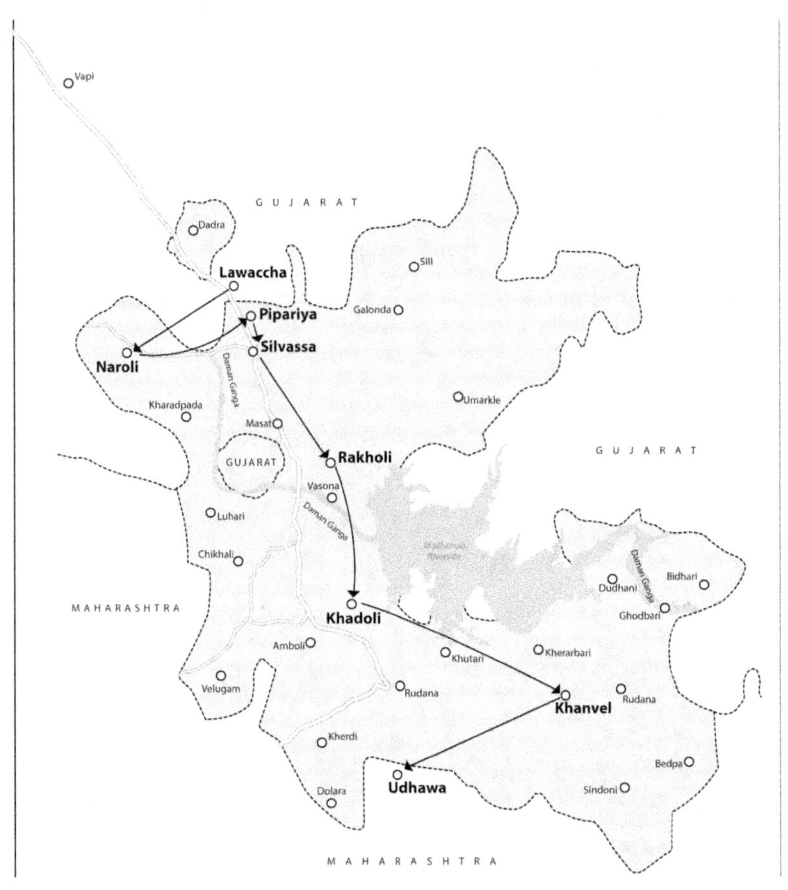

Map indicating the route taken by the volunteers during the course of battle as well as the route taken by Fidaldo during his retreat

Contents

Contents

Foreword

THE impact of Gandhi's Satyagraha was such that most children in independent India grow up believing that non-violent resistance was the sole reason for the success of the freedom struggle. As a result, the role of those who took up arms to free the country from foreign domination has long been side-lined in public memory.

When we think of armed resistance, it's Subhash Chandra Bose and the Indian National Army (INA), Bhagat Singh, Raj Guru, Sukhdev, Chandrashekhar Azad, Khudiram Bose, Master Da and Madan Lal Dhingra who come to mind, amongst others. However, neither the INA, the Hindustan Republican army, nor the sailors or the members of the Chittagong uprising, despite making heroic efforts, succeeded in directly meeting their objectives through the use of arms. This book tells the story of the only rebellion that did.

How I came upon the story and how its many layers revealed themselves constitutes a whole other tale, which I have outlined at the end of this book. A large number of people contributed to the telling, and I am humbled by their belief in my ability to do it. Each one gave me a piece of the truth, which I merely knitted together into a linear narrative.

The very first thank you goes to my publisher Karthika V.K., who first listened to my summary of the story during an event we were at together and took an instant interest in it. One coffee session later, she was committed to the book. It was her idea that I treat the subject seriously, like an amateur historian rather than a storyteller, which was quite scary initially because I find it hard to be serious about anything for more than a few minutes at a time. But with her help, I did it. She pointed me in the right direction, painstakingly read the many drafts of the manuscript and made innumerable vital structural suggestions, all of which added immeasurable value to the manuscript. More than anything else, she became a friend. Thank you for everything, Karthika.

A huge thank you and a hug also to my editor, Sanjana. Her enthusiasm was infectious, and her commitment outstanding. If the flow of the narrative works, it's because of Karthika, and if the script is tight, it's because of Sanjana—god forbid anyone ever read the first draft I wrote before these two worked on it.

A shoutout, too, to everyone at the Westland Delhi office for their warmth and friendship. Thank you for making me feel at home every time I visit.

The most significant source of information for me were the volunteers from Pune who participated in the uprising. Shri Arvind Manolkar and his son Mayuresh Manolkar have been my biggest supporters in this journey. Since our first encounter on a train three years ago, we have met numerous times, and each occasion has brought us closer; now, we are almost family. Many thanks also to Vasantrao Prasade and Dhananjay Shahane for their steadfast support. I was also fortunate to get the help of the Late Padma Vibhushan Babasaheb Purandare, who unfortunately passed on at the age of 100 before the book could be completed. His inputs at our first meeting helped unravel how arms were procured for the uprising. Please bless the book, Babasaheb.

Thanks also to Shreedhar Phadke and Sanjay Vaidya for sharing personal details about their parents' participation in the struggle. Thank you, Shirish Wakankar, for sending me your father's book, which gave me invaluable insights into Rajabhau Wakankar's life.

I had no contacts in Goa and no means of getting information about the Azad Gomantak Dal and its contribution to the struggle. Thank you, Diana Charles, for forwarding my request for help to all your groups and following up until I got the contact I needed. Thank you, Deepa Kamat, for getting me the most valuable contact from Goa—Prabhakar Sinari himself. It was an honour and a privilege to be in the presence of one of the leading lights of the struggle. Despite being unwell, he spent two hours with me. Sir, the autographed copy of your book which you gave me will remain a treasured possession.

Medha Lawande Raikar and Shefali Vaidya, thank you for giving me rare copies of books about your fathers, which shed light on the Azad Gomantak Dal and its activities.

I landed in Silvassa, the main venue of the conflict, with nothing but a telephone number. Yet, I managed to visit the venues where various skirmishes took place and spent two days roaming the jungles and talking to tribals who had fought in the final battle. This was all thanks to Deepak Jadhav, who spent five full days with me and Sarita, drove us around, and put his contacts and political machinery at our disposal so we could get the relevant information. Thank you very much, Deepak Bhai, and please convey my gratitude to your entire team.

A large number of friends have heard this story from me. Each time they said, 'Oh, what a super story!' or 'Why haven't we heard of this before?' it increased my resolve to write it in the best possible way. Thank you, guys.

The book is dedicated to my companion and best friend, my wife Sarita, whose commitment to it has been even greater than mine. My daughters Apoorvaa and Aakanksha were significantly invested in it too, and egged me on to complete it at the earliest. My sons-in-law Rohit and Ashok were constantly updated on progress on the book, as it came up frequently during family dinners. Thank you, team!

Vivasvaan, Anay and Adhitri, here is something to remember your grandfather by. Read it when you are a little older.

16 August 1961

T HERE was silence when Shantibhai Desai, the sarpanch of the Varishtha Panchayat, called out the man's name. He rose and walked slowly towards the dais. With every step that he took, K.G. Badlani, an officer of the Indian Administrative Service (IAS), was conscious that he was making history. He was doing something no civil servant had ever done before. He was about to take an oath to assume office as the prime minister of a country different from his own.

The twenty-one legislators seated in the central square of Silvassa opposite a colonial-era building (one that formerly housed the offices of the Portuguese chief of police) applauded him every step of the way. Just a day before, on 15 August 1961, they had unanimously passed a resolution requesting him to take over as their country's prime minister for twenty-four hours.

As prime minister of the Free State of Dadra and Nagar Haveli, Badlani had only one task to accomplish—to sign away his country's independence so it could merge with India. It was the moment every citizen of Dadra and Nagar Haveli had been waiting for since 15 August 1954, when a group of volunteers under the banner of the Azad Gomantak Dal had overthrown Portuguese rule and established an independent government.

Once the formalities of the oath-taking ceremony were completed, Badlani shook hands with a representative of the Indian government and signed the document that had been kept in readiness. With this, as per the tenth amendment to the Indian Constitution, the Free State of Dadra and Nagar Haveli became a Union Territory of India.[1]

As Desai hoisted the tricolour on the flagpole on which the Portuguese flag had fluttered until 2 August 1954, a cheer went up from the crowd. Shouts of 'Inquilab Zindabad!' and 'Bharat Mata ki Jai!' rent the air.

With the merger, the residents of Silvassa, as well as the Warli and Kokna tribals from the surrounding villages who had gathered to witness the ceremony, achieved a sense of closure. The battle against Portuguese oppression had been won in August 1954, but it was only now, a full seven years later, that they could be sure the war had ended. At last, the saga of cruelty and inhuman excesses that had begun 171 years ago was behind them.

It was also a kind of closure for the Indian nation. With the ouster of the Portuguese from Goa, Daman and Diu and the merger of the Free State of Dadra and Nagar Haveli, the length and breadth of the country was free from European domination. Perhaps it was fitting that the Portuguese, the first foreigners to set up a base in India, were also the last to leave.

---

1   The Constitution (Tenth Amendment) Act, 1961, National Portal of India, https://www.india.gov.in/my-government/constitution-india/amendments/constitution-india-tenth-amendment-act-1961.

Arrival

THE European domination of the Indian subcontinent began with the discovery of the sea route to India by the Portuguese explorer Vasco da Gama. Landing on the Malabar coast on 20 May 1498, he obtained a letter of concession from the Zamorin, the ruler of Calicut, but could not pay the customs duty that all traders were expected to. The Zamorin is said to have held a few of his agents captive, and in response, Vasco da Gama kidnapped some local fishermen and petty officials and decamped to Portugal. Although he failed to establish a base in India, he opened the eyes of the Europeans to its wealth, coming back with goods worth sixty times the cost of the expedition, which had been sponsored by the Portuguese king, Manuel I.

The next significant Portuguese visitor to India was Pedro Alvares Cabral, in 1500. He established a trading post in Calicut, which suffered extensive damage in an attack supposedly instigated by rival Arab merchants. In retaliation, Cabral bombarded Calicut for a whole day. A year later, he returned to Portugal after a rough journey, with only four of the thirteen ships he had left with.

In 1502, Vasco da Gama undertook a second expedition to India and revisited Calicut. He established a trading post and commissioned the building of a fort at Pulicat before returning to Portugal in 1503. In 1505, Fransisco de Almeida was appointed the viceroy of India by Manuel I and despatched with a fleet of twenty-two vessels and 1,500 men. He took up residence in Cochin, from where he governed the territories under his control. He strengthened Fort Manuel and, after many battles and treaties with local rulers, began the construction of a fort at Quilon and another in Cannanore.

Afonso de Albuquerque succeeded Almeida in 1509. A year later, he aligned with Timmayya, a privateer who served the Vijayanagara Empire, to defeat the sultan of Bijapur and establish a permanent settlement at Velha Goa (Old Goa),[2] which served as the headquarters of the Portuguese in India until their ouster in 1961.

The period between 1509 and 1538 was one of steady expansion for the Portuguese in India under various governors and viceroys. This included another stint for Vasco da Gama starting in September 1524, albeit one that was short-lived— he died in Cochin in December 1524.

Under Nuno da Cunha, who was appointed governor in 1529, the Portuguese seized territories from the sultans of Gujarat on the western coast. They took Daman in 1531, Salsette, Bombay, Baçaim in 1534 and Diu in 1535. By the end of the century, the Portuguese controlled large swathes of territory on the western coast of India and a few enclaves

---

2   The most famous church in Goa, the Basilica of Bom Jesus, which houses the remains of St Francis Xavier, is located in Velha.

on the eastern coast. Trade became immensely profitable and stories about the wealth of the East began spreading across the rest of Europe.

The next European power to target India were the Dutch. They landed in 1605 and quickly established trading stations in Calicut. They seized Ceylon from the Portuguese in 1656 and drove them out of the Coromandel coast in 1621, confining them to the areas adjoining their headquarters in the north of Goa. The Dutch then established control over some areas in Bengal and, in 1627, took over Surat. Till the early nineteenth century, they enjoyed a near monopoly over the spice trade.

In 1618, the first Danish East India Company was founded, but it went bankrupt in 1648. A second Danish East India Company was formed in 1670—it too went bankrupt in 1729 when King Frederick IV defaulted on a loan he had taken from the company. A third company, the Danish Asiatic Company, was formed in 1732 and succeeded in stabilising trade substantially. It gained from the wars in Europe between England, France and Holland because each required the services of a neutral country to safely transport its merchandise without the others getting to it. Oddly, the Danes also gained from the growth of the British and French East India Companies. As their influence expanded, British and French officers began misusing their power and indulging in corrupt practices, including using the Danish company to launder their ill-gotten wealth. These funds bolstered its cash flow until the beginning of the nineteenth century. The windfall ended when, in 1799, the British objected to the rights of a neutral nation to carry out trade with foreign colonies to which it did not normally have access during peacetime. In simpler terms, Britain was trying to thwart Denmark from carrying out the trade of countries the former was in conflict with. At the end of the Napoleonic Wars, the British were in a strengthened position, which led to their taking control of all the Danish posts in India one by one, starting with Serampore in 1839. The Danes finally sold their last outpost of Tranquebar[3] to the British in the mid-nineteenth century before departing for good.

The British East India Company then set up a factory in Masulipatnam on the eastern coast of India in 1611 and the following year, established a second one in Surat with a grant of rights by Emperor Jahangir. They obtained permission from the kingdom of Vijayanagar in 1640 and started a third trading post in Madras. By 1647, the East India Company had twenty-three factories across India. In 1661, the Portuguese handed Bombay over to the British Crown, along with the surrounding territories. The Bombay Presidency, as it would later be called, played a crucial role in expanding the company's footprint in India and reducing the influence of the Marathas, the preeminent ruling power at the time.

The French were the last European power to enter India. Francois Caron landed on the coast in 1688 and established the first French factory in Surat. Additional bases came up in Masulipatnam in 1669 and Chandernagore in 1672. In 1673, the French acquired the sleepy fishing village of Pondicherry and made it their headquarters. Under Francois Dupleix, who took over as governor in 1741, they became more ambitious and gained control of the area between Hyderabad and Cape Comorin. Robert Clive shattered their colonial dreams when the Indian faction supported by him defeated the faction backed by the French in the Second Carnatic War (1749–

---

3   Tranquebar, now called Thangambadi, is located just south of Puducherry on the eastern coast. It has the only Danish-era buildings in India and is also where the first printing press in India was set up.

54). After this defeat, Dupleix was dismissed and recalled to France.

The French then incited Nawab Siraj ud-Daulah to attack Fort William in 1757, which led to his rout at the hands of Clive. French influence waned even further. Attempts to regain lost ground came to nought following a rout in the battle of Wandiwash in 1758 and the siege of Pondicherry in 1760. Some territories such as Pondicherry, Chandernagore, Karaikal, Mahe and Yanam were returned to the French by the British in accordance with treaties signed in the aftermath of the Napoleonic Wars. However, French influence in India did not extend beyond these areas.

As a consequence of the arrival of the other European powers and the increasing might of the British East India Company, Portuguese influence remained restricted to Goa, Daman and Diu, which they had held since 1535. The only addition was the territory of Dadra and Nagar Haveli, whose seventy-two villages came under Portuguese control in the period between 1776 and 1783.[4]

---

4   Dr Shimran Khan, *Annexation of Dadra and Nagar Haveli,* Sumit Enterprises, New Delhi, 2019, pp. 78–83.

Expansion

THE takeover of the territories of Dadra and Nagar Haveli began with negotiations over compensation for the *Santana*, a Portuguese warship with 120 sailors and forty cannons that had been captured by the Maratha general Janoji Dhulap in 1772. The Portuguese had asked the ruler, Peshwa Madhav Rao I,[5] to return the vessel to them, but the request was turned down. The matter rested there until 1776 when, taking advantage of the weakening of the Maratha empire, the Portuguese resurrected their demand.[6]

It was a difficult period for the Maratha confederacy. First, Ahmad Shah Abdali delivered them a crushing defeat in the

---

5   The Peshwas were hereditary prime ministers of the Maratha kings—essentially the de facto rulers of the Maratha empire. The most glorious period of the Maratha empire was under Peshwa Baji Rao, who succeeded his father as Peshwa in 1720 and expanded the boundaries of the empire right up to Delhi.

6   Moreshwar Joshi, *Sangram*, Manohar Sadashiv Nirgude, Pune, 1995, p. 19.

Third Battle of Panipat in 1761—an entire generation was wiped out. Additionally, Peshwa Madhav Rao I, who had single-handedly stabilised the empire and was responsible for the turnaround in Maratha fortunes, died in 1772 at the age of twenty-seven. His demise set up a feud for the title of Peshwa that would eventually cost the Marathas their supremacy.

On the death of Madhavrao, his uncle Raghunathrao Bhat, or Raghoba Dada, staked his claim to be appointed the next Peshwa. However, when Shivaji III, the titular head of the Maratha confederacy, appointed Madhavrao's sixteen-year-old brother Narayanrao as the next Peshwa instead, Raghoba had him brutally murdered and assumed the title of Peshwa anyway, which is how such matters were usually settled in those days. As one of the versions of the legend goes, Raghoba sent a note to the head of a gang of mercenaries he employed which read 'Narayanrao na dharave' (arrest Narayanrao). His ambitious second wife Anandibai used a bit of kohl to change the alphabet 'dha' in 'dharave' to 'ma', making it 'marave' or kill. Upon being chased by the mercenaries, Narayanrao rushed to Raghoba, shouting, 'Kaka, mala vachava,' (Uncle, save me). Instead of saving him, Raghoba coldly observed the teenager being brutally stabbed to death.[7]

Disturbed by this act, which was against the ethos of the Maratha court, twelve associates loyal to Madhav Rao I, later collectively called the Barbhais or twelve brothers, sought to make things right. When Raghoba was away fighting the Nizam, they gathered their forces, engaged his troops at Kasegaon and defeated them in 1774. They then installed the five-year-old son of Narayanrao, Madhav Rao II, as the

---

7   Uday S. Kulkarni, *The Maratha Century*, Mula Mutha Publishers, Pune, 2021, pp. 178–179.

Peshwa, with Nana Fadnavis (born Balaji Janardan Bhanu) as his advisor.[8] Nana steered the Maratha confederacy through a long and challenging period but could not save it from the internal conflicts stemming mainly from Raghoba's hunger for the title of Peshwa.

After the defeat of his forces at Kasegaon, Raghoba sought refuge with the British East India Company, promising them territories in return for their aid in defeating his grand-nephew's army. Nana immediately despatched a letter to the company, requesting their support. The company sent their representative to Fort Purandar, where the young Peshwa resided, and signed the first treaty of Purandar, by which they agreed to hand over Raghoba.

But soon afterwards, Governor-General Warren Hastings expressed dissatisfaction with the terms of the treaty and threatened to go to war. The Barbhais, fully aware of the danger posed by a combined army of the British and Raghoba, swiftly acquiesced to a revised second treaty, ceding the territories promised to the company by Raghoba, and asked again that he be handed over to them.[9]

Meanwhile, the French sent an ambassador to the court of the Peshwa, even as the Anglo–French wars were being fought in southern and eastern India. Accusing the Marathas of fraternising with the enemy, Hastings once more reneged on the treaty's terms and sent his forces towards Pune. In the first Anglo–Maratha war, fought near Talegaon in May 1779, the British were soundly thrashed and Raghoba was finally returned to the Marathas' custody by the terms of a new and final treaty. Many of the territories the company had wrested

---

8   Kulkarni, p. 185.
9   Joshi, p. 19.

via the second treaty of Purandar reverted to the Marathas, leaving the British smarting.

The Marathas treated Raghoba with respect, as deserving of a son of the valiant Bajirao Peshwa, and after extracting an undertaking from him that he would stay away from Pune, released him. He, however, broke his word and sought shelter with the Portuguese.

The Portuguese took advantage of the fact that the Marathas would not want to fight them so soon after clashing with the British. Raghoba's arrival strengthened their position and they demanded compensation for the *Santana*—an issue that had been on the back-burner for well over six years. Governor José Pedro da Câmara, as the representative of Queen Maria the Pious, proposed a treaty with the Peshwa, the terms of which were negotiated by Narayan Vithal Dhume, specially loaned for this task by the Nizam of Hyderabad. The treaty proposed a permanent peace and standing together as allies against common enemies, but the signal was clear—agree to our terms or we will add to your troubles by siding with your foes. With Raghoba's associates, including his adoptive son Amrut Rao, seeking to bring him back, the British East India Company waiting to avenge its defeat and the Nizam preparing to attack their southern flanks, Nana knew the Marathas could not afford another enemy, so he advised the Peshwa to accept the terms.

On the surface, the treaty espoused standing together against mutual adversaries, an agreement to not shelter fugitives in each other's territories and allowing ships safe access to ports controlled by both parties. But it was really about releasing Raghoba to the Marathas in return for compensation in the form of ₹56,544 in cash, teakwood worth ₹3,000 (enough to build a ship) and saranjam (revenue collection rights) to territories in the provinces adjoining

Daman.[10] Unknown to either party, the term 'saranjam' would whip up a storm in the International Court of Justice in 1960 and help decide the future of the territories involved.

Sixty-five villages of Dadra and Nagar Haveli were ceded in all by the Marathas. Three years later, the Portuguese bought the remaining seven from the raja of Jawhar, establishing complete hegemony over the area. The seventy-two villages, spread over 491 square kilometres and with a population of less than 20,000, yielded a revenue of ₹12,000 per annum. Daman, where the governor was based, and the adjoining territories were categorised broadly into the districts of Damasco Grande, Naeer, Dadra and Nagar Haveli.

Daman was a coastal town with a large garrison of Portuguese soldiers which could be bolstered by reinforcements arriving through the sea route from Goa and Diu. Dadra and Nagar Haveli were landlocked, separated from each other by a narrow strip of land, and Nagar Haveli was further separated from Daman by a thirty-five-kilometre region ruled by the raja of Dharampur. Since the raja was friendly with the Portuguese, they did not feel the need to take it over. The Portuguese territory was under the control of an administrator based in Silvassa, who reported to the governor in Daman. A chief of police and a judge were the only other Portuguese officials posted in Silvassa; the others were recruited from among the locals.

The region was bisected by the rain-fed Daman Ganga River and consisted mainly of jungles interrupted by the occasional settlement, with Silvassa being the largest. The Daman Ganga's tributaries—Shrimant, Val, Rayte, Lendi, Vagh, Sakartond, Dongarkhedi, Roshni, Dudhni—swelled into huge, fast-flowing waterways during the monsoons. The

---

10   Joshi, p. 19.

jungles, which housed most of the tribal populace, comprised deciduous trees with teak, sandra, mahara and khair, bled into bordering territories such as Gujarat and Maharashtra.

Being the only territory under Portuguese occupation without direct access to the sea would alter the course of the enclave's history—a fact that, naturally, nobody could have foreseen.[11]

The Dhodia, Kokna and Warli tribals, who constituted almost 80 per cent of the new district's population, lived in small villages (called 'padas') within the lush jungles. Each pada typically consisted of a few ramshackle huts built around a central square and had a shrine to Waghdev, the local deity. Extreme poverty was the order of the day. Except for the other 20 per cent of the population, which included landlords and their cohorts, many of whom had been appointed Patels or revenue collectors by the Portuguese.

Already leading miserable lives, the tribals had no idea that things were going to become worse. If someone had told them so, they would probably have laughed and taken another swig of the country liquor their Patels supplied them with so liberally.[12]

---

11   Joshi, pp. 21–22.
12   Conversation with Deepak Jadhav, political worker.

Exploitation

THE tribals of the Nagar Haveli jungles had never known what plenty was, though what they had was adequate.

The more affluent among them had small plots of land to till, although these plots grew smaller with each passing generation as they were divided between brothers. In the good years, the single crops of nangli and arahar (finger millet and a pulse, respectively) that they produced, even after the chauth (tax) the Patel[13] took away, lasted them through most of the year. They had hens and goats, so milk and eggs were aplenty, and they could hunt if food fell short. On good days, when someone managed to snare a fat hare or a deer, the entire community would rejoice, drink, dance under the banyan tree and thank Waghdev for the life they had. When the rains

---

13   A Patel was a revenue collector who kept a share of the revenue collected as his fee and passed on the rest to the governing power. They were often influential landlords and also maintained land records which gave them immense power as they could take away or allot lands.

failed, they managed to survive by working in the fields of the Patels and the landlords, whose areas were irrigated with water from the Daman Ganga River.

All this changed when the fanaga, or foreigner, came. The Patels suddenly started demanding half the crop as chauth, claiming that it was the law of the fanaga. In reality, the Portuguese had little interest in the territories and maintained only a skeletal presence, relying entirely on the Patels for revenue collection. Given a free rein, the Patels began to exploit the tribals and appropriate the tiny parcels of land they owned.

The standard procedure was to understate the produce from their own fields, overstate that of the small tribal landowners and extract taxes from them. The tribals ended up giving away almost the entire crop they had grown and ran out of grain within a few days of harvesting. The Patels would then 'lend' them grain to tide them over the lean period and demand twice that amount back during the next harvest in a system referred to as 'khavti'. Obviously, few could abide by such terms; those who could not were beaten up and lost their houses, families and lands. All they had to help them through rough times was the country liquor they brewed. Entire populations, it is said, succumbed to alcoholism.

Daman continued to thrive because it was the main centre for importing opium and almost all the Portuguese officers had a stake in the illicit trade. There was no such attraction in Dadra and Nagar Haveli, so visits by officers to Silvassa were rare. When they did visit, the Patels and the landlords would wine and dine their benefactors and send them back with handsome gifts. The chicken and mutton they feasted on came from the tribals, as did the girls who were summoned for 'entertainment'.

As soon as the Patels' men entered a village, accompanied by the odd Portuguese soldier clad in khaki shorts and a shirt, a shout would go up: 'Pada re pada, fanaga aala re!' (Run, run, the firangi has come!). The villagers would gather up what they could and flee into the jungle, leaving their doorless hovels for the outsiders to plunder to their heart's content.

With their small parcels of land being seized by the landlords in lieu of grain, most of the tribals were left without any possessions to call their own. Many left their villages to work in the cities of British India. While the young worked, the elders begged and died on the streets, far from their beloved hamlets and jungles.

During the famine of 1859, most of the able-bodied men left for the cities. The following year, the Patels had no one to work on their fields, and when harvest season came, the entire district was barren. Revenues plummeted.

Having been repeatedly hit where it hurt them the most, the Portuguese sought to remedy the situation. A reform committee was set up in 1870, consisting of a senior Patel, a local officer and an officer from Goa. The committee reviewed the plots of land the Patels had misappropriated and returned some to their original owners. Another committee was set up in 1878, which surveyed and reallocated parcels of farmland. With some order restored, the tribals began to trickle back home and agricultural trade blossomed. Soon, Dadra and Nagar Haveli were supplying rice, eggs, poultry, mutton and firewood to the entire Daman province.

This new-found prosperity provided only a brief respite from exploitation since it drew greater interest from the Portuguese officers in the district. The number of police posts, border checkpoints and supervising officers multiplied almost overnight. Suddenly, the fanaga were everywhere. The exploitation and the beatings, which had never really stopped, intensified. The parasitic landlords lived off the tribals, who gradually sank back into abject poverty. They were forced to work in the fields as bonded labourers—stories abounded of sick men being dragged out of their houses and sent to the landlords' farms. The women—easy targets for the landlords and their hangers-on—were ruthlessly exploited. Having tribal concubines became the norm, and women were discarded and replaced at will.

When there was less work on the farms, the landlords made the tribals cut jungle grass, bind it into fifty-pound bales and load these into carts. Sometimes, the men were yoked to the carts and made to pull them. All they got in return were two or three annas, whereas the landlords made profits of up to ₹20 a bale.

The landlords lived in huge houses with well-manicured lawns while their tribal servants were housed in squalor. They maintained luxurious holiday homes in Mumbai and Goa and took a keen interest in the officers who were posted to Silvassa. These landlords were a mix of Parsis, Hindus, Muslims and Iranis, and though their religion distinguished how they lived, the one thing common to them all was their contempt for the tribals. They left all the dirty work to hired supervisors and their goons, all of whom shared the view that the tribals were mere beasts of burden.

The supervisors enforced fourteen-hour work days, disallowing even toilet breaks, and dealt with any drop in productivity, as defined by them and regardless of reason, with a stern hand. Workers were beaten mercilessly, at times without cause, merely to 'set an example'. The multi-tailed whip was a standard issue for all supervisors, who applied it liberally on the bare backs of men and women alike. A common punishment the men suffered was having their long braids tied to their feet and standing in the sun in awkward, contorted positions while their backsides were lashed. Sometimes they were left bound to a tree for hours without food or water or hung upside down from the branches and beaten soundly. The Patels often made them put their thumbprints on documents they did not understand, then used these to accuse them of theft and throw them into jail. A few who protested were burnt alive by the landlord's accomplices.

Once again, the old warning began to echo through the tribal villages: 'Pada re pada, fanaga aala re!' And once again, they gathered whatever they could before fleeing into the jungles.[14]

---

14   Godavari Parulekar, trans. Nikhil Gavankar, *The Awakening of Man*, Popular Prakashan, Mumbai, 2015, pp. 20–50.

First Whiff of Independence

THE British East India Company ruled as a sovereign power until the Indian Rebellion of 1857, after which the Crown of England took over all its territories. Similarly, in 1769, the loss-making French East India Company was dissolved and King Louis VI issued an edict transferring its assets to the Crown. In return, he took care of all the debts the company had incurred and wrote off the deficit. Both the British and French enterprises were initially joint stock companies and, therefore, partially insulated from the impact of political changes in the home countries.

In contrast, the Portuguese expeditions were funded directly by the Crown, and any territories or resources acquired in India were considered assets of the Portuguese state. The administration of Portuguese territories in India was consequently impacted by conditions back home. And unlike in England, the political situation in Portugal was volatile.

This wasn't always the case. When Vasco da Gama first landed in India, Portugal was ruled by King Manuel I—a direct descendant (though of a different line) of King Afonso I, who founded the state of Portugal. During his twenty-six-year rule, Brazil was colonised and Portuguese expeditions reached what is now Canada. Trading posts were established in countries as far apart as India, Indonesia, Timor, Taiwan, Muscat and Japan.

From 1580 to 1640, Portugal was in a dynastic union with Spain, as a result of which it lost control of its foreign policy. It ventured into the eighty-year Dutch–Portuguese war, during which several of its colonies were seized by the Dutch. This union ended in 1640 when John IV fought the Restoration War and founded the house of Braganza, which ruled Portugal till 1910.

In 1807, the Napoleonic Wars saw France invade Portugal. King John VI shifted base to Brazil and declared it an independent country. After the defeat of Napoleon in 1815, Portugal was ruled by a regent controlled by the British, who had helped the Portuguese fight France. The Liberal Revolution of 1820 restored the monarchy and King John VI returned to Portugal, leaving his son Pedro in charge of Brazil. There were several skirmishes and internal conflicts in the years that followed, until 1910, when, in the aftermath of a revolt, the monarchy was abolished and a republican government took its place.

Given the political upheavals within the country, the Portuguese found it difficult to expand their territory in India, remaining confined to small coastal holdings such as Goa, Diu and Panikota. It was during this period, for a brief while between 1835–1837, that the residents of Daman, Dadra and Nagar Haveli had the first independent government.[15]

---

15   Khan, pp. 18–27.

The five ships set off from Bombay harbour for Goa on 27 May 1835. About 300 sailors, commanded by Admiral Hillbrow, had been recruited from among the Goan exiles settled in Konkan, Belgaum, Dharwad and the surrounding areas. This navy of the provisional government of Portuguese-controlled territories based in Daman had three clear goals: attack Goa, depose the Portuguese viceroy and restore Dr Bernando Peres da Silva as the governor.

Dr Peres da Silva was a medical practitioner and an ethnic Goan who had become popular when he exposed the corruption that was rife in the Goan healthcare service. He then led an insurrection against the viceroy, the Count of Rio Padro, and deposed him. In 1822, when the Portuguese Indian territories were allowed to elect members to the Portuguese parliament, da Silva contested against the local whites and the *mestiço* (mixed parentage) candidates and won the election, but was unable to execute his duties because, even before he could reach Lisbon, Parliament was dissolved and monarchy restored in Portugal. He was elected once more in 1827 but had to flee into exile in England and later Brazil, when King Miguel I briefly took over and appointed his own men to the posts in Portuguese India.

Then, in 1834, when Prince Pedro of Brazil ousted King Miguel I and placed his daughter on the throne, da Silva was appointed *prefeito* (prefect) of Portuguese India. This was partly because of his son's closeness to Pedro, in whose armies he had fought.

Da Silva took office on 14 January 1835 and initiated many reforms at breakneck speed in an attempt to clean up the system. However, the army, consisting primarily of whites and mestiços, resented these reforms and he was overthrown after just eighteen days. In the battle that followed, his supporters were pushed back to Fort Gaspar Dias (Fort Terekhol) in north Goa. The militarists, led by Viceroy Manuel de Portugal e Castro, massacred the lot of them, hung their severed heads from the fort's ramparts and snuffed out the only people-friendly regime the region had known for centuries.

Da Silva escaped first to Mumbai and then to Daman, where the locals welcomed him as a hero and, under his leadership, formed the first independent state of Daman, Diu, Dadra and Nagar Haveli. He then raised funds from the British and some friends in Mumbai and set off for Goa with five ships, ready for battle. Unfortunately, as per a report, the five ships met with choppy seas and, on 6 June 1836, supposedly sank off the coast of Goa. With them sank the Goan people's hope of freedom from Portuguese rule.[16]

The provisional government that da Silva headed remained in existence until 1837. However, the bureaucracy, observing a decline in his power, began to sabotage his plans and switched loyalties to the regime in Goa. The British, too, withdrew support and the friends who had lent him money asked for it to be returned. At that point, some say he made peace with the governor, and returned to Goa, while others say he was arrested and exiled. There are also reports that he returned to Portugal and continued to be active in politics as a representative of Goa, even being re-elected to parliament twice before passing away in 1844, in Lisbon. In any case, the Goan military regained control of Dadra and Nagar Haveli in 1837, and the brief flirtation with freedom died an ignoble death. The old regime of the landlords and the fanaga was re-established and continued unchallenged for well over a century.[17]

---

16   Joshi, p. 22.
17   Khan, pp. 15–23.

Obdurance

O N 3 June 1947, Lord Mountbatten, the last British viceroy of India, formally proposed the division of India into two sovereign countries—India and Pakistan. What followed was tragedy on an unprecedented scale, with lakhs of people killed and many more displaced on both sides of the border. As per the 1951 census of India and Pakistan—carried out four years after partition—Pakistan identified 72,26,600 displaced persons whilst India identified 72,95,870.[18]

The newly formed Indian government also had to grapple with its inheritance of a fractured country. Though the British had exercised control over most parts of India, they had not administered all of it directly. 'British India' consisted of the many princely states which had been annexed by the East India Company or the Crown, as well as those seized from other

---

18 Prashant Bharadwaj, Asim Khwaja, Atif Mian, 'The Big March: Migratory Flows after the Partition Of India', Harvard Kennedy School Faculty Research Working Paper Series, June 2008, HKS Working Paper No. RWP08-029, https://ssrn.com/abstract=1124093.

European powers. Some princely states had ceded control to the British but were administered autonomously. When India became independent in 1947, there were approximately 84 princely states in existence, covering roughly 40 per cent of India's geographical area and containing about 28 per cent of its population. Under the Indian Independence Act of 1947, they were given the choice of joining India or Pakistan or staying independent.

Of the occupying powers, the Danes and the Dutch had already left India long before the start of the twentieth century. With the departure of the British, only the French and the Portuguese remained. At the time of independence, the French controlled roughly 510 square kilometres of territory, of which 293 square kilometres were in Pondicherry. They ceded their lodges in Machilipatnam, Kozhikode and Surat to India on 6 October 1947. An agreement was signed between France and India in 1948, according to which elections would take place in the Indian territories controlled by the French—the idea was to allow the people to choose their own political future. When they voted overwhelmingly in favour of joining India, the French ceded the governance of Chandernagore to India on 2 May 1950, after which it was merged with the state of West Bengal on 2 October 1954. On 1 November 1954, the four enclaves of Pondichéry, Yanam, Mahe and Karikal were informally handed over to the Indian union, becoming the Union Territory of Puducherry, although the legally-recognised union of French India with India did not occur until 1962, which is when the French parliament ratified the treaty with India. Their departure was, therefore, peaceful and carried out with mutual agreement.[19]

---

19   Ajit Niyogi, 'Decolonization of French India: Liberation Movement and Indo French Relations 1947-1954', Institut Francais de Pondichery, Pondicherry, 1997.

At the beginning of 1954, the only territories not under the control of the Indian government, besides the French enclaves, were the Portuguese enclaves of Goa, Daman, Diu, Dadra and Nagar Haveli. Although the Portuguese presence in India was fairly nominal, the Indian government did not attempt to liberate the territories from their control. This inaction was due to changes in the political situation in Portugal and their implications for India.

On 1 February 1908, republican activists had assassinated King Dom Carlos I and Prince Royal Luís Filipe in Lisbon. The king's younger son, Manuel II, took the throne but was overthrown in 1910, after which the monarchy was abolished and the second republican government came to power.

Over the next fifteen years, Portugal went through forty-five governments in rapid succession and endured economic chaos. Participation in World War I further weakened the economy. On 28 May 1926, the Ditadura Nacional (National Dictatorship) seized power in another coup.[20] General Manuel Gomes da Costa, the coup's leader, became the president but was dethroned by General António Oscar de Fragoso Carmona, who assumed the designations of both president and prime minister—for good measure, one must suppose. In February 1928, the Comissão de Propaganda da Ditadura (Commission for the Propaganda of the Dictatorship) was created. Carmona organised a presidential election on 25 March 1928, in which he was the only candidate, and was duly 'elected' for a five-year term as president.

In 1930, Antonio de Oliveira Salazar was made prime minister and in 1933, he established the Estado Nova (the New State), which defined Portugal as a single-party multi-continent country (spread across Europe, Africa, Asia

---

20   Khan, pp. 23–24.

and Oceania). This meant that Portuguese territories in India were an integral part of the Portuguese state. Since Portugal was a founding member of the North Atlantic Treaty Organisation (NATO), any military action against the Portuguese territories in India, it was feared, might result in a confrontation with NATO member-nations.[21]

This is why the government of India, having neither the strength nor the inclination to take on NATO, did not initiate any action to liberate the territories. The Portuguese, secure in this knowledge, let loose a reign of terror against the local population. Discontent rose. Satyagraha and other tools of peaceful protest, which had worked so well against the British, cut no ice with the Portuguese, who countered every demonstration with extreme violence. With the Indian government unable and unwilling to act, it was left to a group of individuals to take the Portuguese on, even if it necessitated the use of violence.

That is where our story truly commences.

---

21 Ibid.

Beginnings

IT was October 1952. Prabhakar Sinari[22] pushed open the door, and before anyone could react, Debu, an accomplice, ran out and headed for the boundary wall of the hospital, the Escola Medico Cirurgica da Goa. The startled guards drinking on the bench a little further down the corridor barely had time to react. As they watched Debu disappear round the corner, Sinari came rushing towards them, shouting, 'To palun gelo, to palun gelo!' He has escaped!

The guards jumped up and rushed towards the fleeing prisoner, then stopped when they heard the scream of the orderly who worked in the prison ward of the hospital. Understanding dawned too slow. Sinari had conned them. The orderly, who had opened the gate to deliver food to the

---

22 Sinari not only played a major role in the liberation of Dadra and Nagar Haveli but also aided the Indian army when it liberated Goa, Daman and Diu in 1961. After 1961, he joined the police service, rose to the rank of inspector-general and played a stellar role during the insurgency in Punjab.

prisoners, was doubled over, his nose bleeding from a vicious punch.

Seeing the short, stocky figure of the twenty-one-year-old Prabhakar Sinari race away in the opposite direction, the cabo knew that his career was over. He had let the most dreaded terrorist, whom the Portuguese government had been planning to transport to Lisbon to serve a thirteen-year jail term, escape. The head constable knew his excuse of being short-staffed due to Diwali was unlikely to pacify his seniors.

He chased after Sinari as fast as he could in his inebriated state while the orderly, clutching his bleeding nose, raised the alarm. Sinari ran towards the boundary wall, then seeing the laboratory building ahead, ducked into it, only to find himself face-to-face with a guard. He kicked him hard in the stomach and ran back to jump over the boundary wall. As bullets whizzed by his head, Sinari dived into the Panjim creek and, after a few short, fierce strokes underwater, emerged some metres away. Four years after being sentenced, he had finally succeeded in breaking out of prison.[23]

This second attempt was nowhere near as dramatic as the first had been—he had jumped from the top of the fifty-metre-high wall of the Reis Magos Fort jail, hoping to land on a garbage pile at the bottom. Instead, misjudging the trajectory, he had collided painfully with a tree and been promptly captured again. He was thrown into solitary confinement, starved, lashed with belts made of hippopotamus leather and denied permission to attend his father's funeral. The crimes that had got him into prison in the first place were the killing

---

23   Prabhakar Sinari, *From Darkness to Dawn: A first-person account of the militant struggle to liberate Goa from Portuguese colonialism*, Golden Heart Emporium Books, Goa, pp. 82–86.

of a guard while attempting to loot the treasury in the Fazenda building in Mapusa as well as a subsequent endeavour to rob the local bank, the Banco Nacional Ultramarino. Though in his teens when sentenced, he was considered a 'threat' to the Portuguese empire in India; a dangerous terrorist.[24]

Sinari disagreed with both terms. He considered himself a freedom fighter waging war on the Portuguese to liberate his motherland and said as much in court during his sentencing, defiantly declaring that he would continue his efforts till Goa was free or till he breathed his last.

Prabhakar Sinari transformed from the carefree son of a local landlord to a fiery revolutionary almost overnight, in June 1946. As a fifteen-year-old student at the Escola Moderna, he had joined a peaceful protest against the arrest of the socialist leader Ram Manohar Lohia in Mapusa, on the urging of his favourite teacher, Sadananad Apu Manapat. He was stunned to see the Portuguese police beating up protestors, even children as young as ten or twelve, with leather belts. When he rushed to save his teacher, he found him lying on the ground in a muddy pool of rainwater. Policemen were kicking him with hobnailed boots. It seemed to Sinari then that the only language the Portuguese understood was aggression, and he vowed to devote his life to the cause of throwing them out using any means necessary.[25]

He joined the Azad Gomantak Dal, the breakaway group of the Goa National Congress which had decided that peaceful protests, which worked well against the British, would not work against the Portuguese. Initially, the Dal considered itself a part of the Congress, its goal being to supplement the party's efforts. However, a core group decided that the time

---

24 Sinari, pp. 76–77.
25 Sinari, pp. 18–19.

for strategic violence was now imminent. It was to a meeting
of this group, led by Vishwanath Lawande, that Sinari headed
in June 1947. The venue of the meeting was the Shantadurga
temple at Kunkoliem, near Ponda.

The temple, deceptively built like a church with exposed
brick walls, sloping roofs and a belfry tower-like structure at
the rear, still houses a shaant or peaceful idol of the goddess
Durga. According to legend, Vishnu and Shiva once got
locked in a fierce battle that threatened to destroy the world.
Brahma then prayed to Durga to step in and establish peace.
She obliged, holding Vishnu with one hand and Shiva with
the other.

Ironically, it was behind this temple of peace that Sinari
took an oath to deliver his land from the Portuguese. A loaded
pistol in his hand, he repeated the words of the Dal oath after
Lawande:

> With an invocation to God and salute to the weapon
> held in my hand, I do, hereby, take the oath and solemnly
> declare that I fully accept the primary objective of a
> speedy deliverance of Indian land from the Portuguese
> occupation. I am aware of the perils and obstacles in the
> path towards Goa's freedom, and I shall extend myself
> to the utmost, unwaveringly, to achieve our ultimate
> aim.[26]

Now, as he emerged for breath in the creek during his second
attempt at escape, Sinari knew that he was in danger of being
recaptured. Police officers would be swarming the streets
searching for him, and were they to find him, the next step
would be deportation to Portugal. Determined not to let that

---

26   Sinari, pp. 43–44.

happen, he plunged back into the murky waters and swam to the other side of the bank. He could see the flashlights, the policemen shooting randomly into the stream, and knew that it was only a matter of time before they summoned speedboats to look for him. To throw them off his scent, he crawled through the tall grass on the river bank in the direction of the jail hospital he had escaped from, instead of away from it. Then, emerging somewhere near the police staff quarters, he hid in a coconut grove to recover his breath and, after a few minutes, stepped out and began the long walk to safety. But a few kilometres away, near the village of Taleigao, trouble awaited.

Seeing the headlights of an approaching vehicle, Sinari waved it down, assuming it was a bus. Unfortunately for him, it was a luxury car transporting two European officers and their guards. Before they could get out of the vehicle, he turned and bolted, only to run straight into the headlights of an approaching motorcycle patrol. Cut off from both sides, he darted into the undergrowth near the creek. When the officers abandoned their motorcycles to come after him, he waded back into the muddy waters. The stream was too shallow for him to swim in, so he squatted and submerged himself, using a lotus stem as a makeshift snorkel. After what seemed like an eternity, he surfaced silently and was relieved to see them trampling through the undergrowth some distance away. Crawling out of the creek once more, Sinari sprinted towards Taleigao.

As he neared the village, he slowed to a walk and began pulling off the leeches that had attached themselves to his body. Hungry, weak and bleeding, he knew he could not possibly make it any further looking as bedraggled as he did. So he took shelter in an empty cowshed he had spotted in the middle of a field and dropped into sleep, exhausted.

A few hours later, he stirred. It was dusk. Thanking the stars that nobody had stumbled upon him, he washed himself at a well, then picked up a bale of hay and, placing it on his head, walked into the village of St Cruz, looking like an ordinary labourer. He made his way to his cousin's house and stayed long enough for a refreshing bath, clean clothes and some other supplies. Then he headed towards Chimbel, where he ate a good meal and rested before sending a message to his family to let them know he had escaped.

On the third day, dressed in a kashti, a short loincloth, with a blanket thrown over his shoulder, Sinari boarded a canoe at Ribandar and made it to Poira, near the Indian border. There, he met Sitaram Ghatwal, an old associate, and stayed in his house till the heat died down.

On the fourth day, Sinari and Ghatwal made their way into the dense jungle along the border at 9 p.m. They had walked close to a kilometre when, suddenly, a Russell's viper crossed their path. Seeing it just in time, the men hopped over the highly venomous snake—it was a close call. Shortly afterwards, they froze upon hearing a leopard's snarl. Although unable to see in the pitch dark, they sensed it was close and hastily clambered up a cashew tree. Nerves jangling, they stayed there and waited for dawn. When the first rays of the sun lit up the jungle, they descended and strode into the village of Maneri in India. Triumphantly throwing aside the blanket on his shoulder, Sinari turned back towards the Portuguese customs post, waved a fist and shouted the most colourful curses he knew.[27] The border guards watched helplessly—he had crossed over into India and was safe from them.

From Maneri, Sinari proceeded to Belgaum, where the Azad Gomantak Dal had an office. Inspired by his presence,

---

27   Sinari, p. 88–94.

the volunteers there decided to launch a major assault on the Portuguese. A target was chosen—the landlocked enclaves of Dadra and Nagar Haveli. And so, the first team of liberators was assembled.[28]

In Pune, the premises of the Hindu Tarun Mandal[29] in Guruwar Peth were overflowing with people who had come to watch the highly contested final of the annual kabaddi tournament. It was so crowded that some had perched themselves on the boundary walls.

The Tarun Mandal had won the last five tournaments by soundly thrashing their opponents, but this time seemed different. The visiting team from Kurundwadi had succeeded in tagging five of the Mandal's players. Only two players were left in the home team, whereas all seven of the opposing team were still in the game. The captain of the Kurundwadi team made the next move. Chanting *huntututu*, he zigzagged skilfully across to the Mandal's side and swiftly tagged one more of the home team. A hush descended on the ground as the crowd realised defeat was imminent. One more unsuccessful raid and they would be out of the reckoning.

Raja Wakankar knew he had no choice. He gestured to the umpire that a substitution was being made and stepped onto the court. His short, squat, muscular body glistened with oil. He bent and smeared soil from the court on his forehead. A roar went up from the crowd and the opposing team

---

28 Sinari, p. 102.

29 Hindu Tarun Mandal was a popular haunt for young men right from its inception before independence. It was particularly known for the kabaddi team. It is still operative and during Ganapati celebrations, its activities increase substantially.

went into a huddle. Their coach hurried over to give them special tips. For Rajabhau Wakankar was everyone's hero, a revered idol. He was the champion of many a tourney and a national-level player. But he was also thirty-three. The other team consisted of twenty-year-olds in peak physical form. How many of them could he tag in one breath? Would the other side fail to tag him when they raided? Even his greatest admirers felt he had little chance. There was a hushed silence all around as Raja prepared to raid.

As he stepped across the line, a steady *hutututututu* emanated from deep within his throat. The opposing team formed a chain and drew him into their centre. As he attempted to tag the player on the extreme left, the entire squad lunged at him, and he seemed to go under. There was pin-drop silence for a second, and then the crowd roared in unison. They had just witnessed a near-miracle. When the team had closed in on Rajabhau, he had stepped onto the shoulder of one of his opponents, jumped over the huddle and sprinted back to his side of the court.

The game was over. Raja had tagged all seven members of the Kurundwadi team in one go. The home team were champions once again.[30]

As his friends lifted him onto their shoulders and carried him around the court, Rajabhau raised his fist and shouted, 'Akhand Bharat!'

The crowd roared back, 'Hokar rahega!'

For Rajabhau Wakankar, these kabaddi games and tournaments were all part of a larger agenda— spreading the message of militant nationalism espoused by the Rashtriya Swayam Sewak Sangh (RSS) and uniting young people for nation-building. As a full-time volunteer for the RSS, it was

---

30   Hemant Jogev, *Dainik Lokmat*, 1999.

his strategy to dazzle youngsters with his physical prowess and then introduce them to his ideology. Born in Sangli, some 250 kilometres south of Pune, he had come into contact with Babarao Savarkar, the older brother of Vinayak Damodar Savarkar, the Hindu nationalist icon, and been drawn to their philosophy. The followers of Savarkar infamously refused to accept the partition of India and looked forward to the day the country would return to its pre-partition status.[31]

The men who gathered around Raja after the crowd had left were some of his closest friends, as close to family as he would ever have in Pune. The tall, muscular Nana Kajrekar from Satara was in his late twenties, built like a bull and forever thirsty for action. The equally tall but slim and bearded Moreshwar Purandare was a history buff; any mention of Shivaji would send him into an adulatory stupor. In stark contrast to both, the soft-spoken Sudhir Phadke had an artistic bent and was just beginning to make his mark as a music director in the Marathi film industry. He was the only one among them who was married and his house was usually where they met, for they could be guaranteed tea and snacks as they discussed the world's affairs.[32]

That December evening in 1953, the men spoke excitedly about the match and Rajabhau's heroic performance before the conversation shifted to politics. A statement made by Prime Minister Jawaharlal Nehru the previous day in Parliament was the trigger. 'The Indian government will not send its forces to liberate Goa,' Nehru had said. 'The Goan people will have to do it themselves.'[33]

---

31   Joshi, pp. 39–40.

32   In conversation with B.M. Purandare, historian, and Shreedhar Phadke.

33   In conversation with B.M. Purandare, historian.

The argument that India was in no position to take on the combined forces of NATO carried no weight with these young hotheads. They took the statement to represent Nehru's desire to bolster his international peacenik image at the cost of people's lives in the occupied territories. They had often discussed the concept of Akhand Bharat (Unified India) with Babarao Savarkar and their gurus in the RSS, Babarao Bhide and Vinayakrao Apte. Each time, they ended with the question—what was the use of talking about Akhand Bharat if parts of India were still not free of foreign domination?

Rajabhau and Purandare had spoken of this with each other, and also with Appasaheb Karmalkar, a father figure for the Azad Gomantak Dal, who lived in exile in Mumbai. They conceded the fact that the Portuguese were too powerful to take on and they did not have the resources to fight them. However, they had always believed that the Indian government would act at some point, and they would then plunge in to offer support.

Nehru's statement put an end to this hope. That evening, the four men swore an oath that resources or no resources, they would wage war with Portugal and liberate the occupied territories. The fight would begin with Dadra and Nagar Haveli, which were landlocked and hence the easiest of all the targets, and then, gathering strength from there, they would take Daman, Diu and Goa.[34]

The second team was now in place.

More than 150 kilometres away, in a small village in a district of Thane, Maharashtra, a sea of faces turned towards

---

34   Joshi, p. 19.

Godavaribai Parulekar as she rose to speak at a rally. It had been many years since the tribals met the couple who had helped liberate them from the tyranny of the Patels and landlords. Godavari and her husband Shamrao, staunch communists, had been banned from entering this district following their imprisonment in 1946.

On their release in 1953, their first halt was the Mahaluxmi village, where thousands of Adivasis gathered to welcome them. Godavari, dressed in her trademark white saree, was overcome with emotion. She turned to her husband, who mirrored her sentiments. 'We are so small compared to this sea of humanity,' he said softly. 'What tremendous loyalty, zeal and capacity for resistance! They have broken the shackles of oppression with their strength. We are merely their instruments.'[35]

Godavari Parulekar, born Godavari Gokhale, was the daughter of Laxman Rao Gokhale, a well-to-do lawyer from Pune. Her father was a supporter of the moderate faction of the Congress party and a cousin of the renowned freedom fighter Gopal Krishna Gokhale. Godavari completed her master's degree in economics from Pune University and went on to become the first woman lawyer in Maharashtra.

Jumping into the freedom struggle early in life, she landed in jail twice. Her father, unhappy with her participation in politics, threw her out of his house. She moved to Bombay, where she joined the Servant's Society of India and later, the Communist Party of India. In 1939, she met and married Shamrao Parulekar, and they plunged into what would become their life's work: helping the Adivasis of Thane and

---

35 Parulekar, p. 113.

Gadchiroli resist the tyranny of the British state and the local landlords.[36]

As she rose to address the crowd, Godavari's mind wandered to an afternoon in 1943 when she had trekked all day to reach Salkar, a pada in the village of Dongri in the Umbargaon region of Maharashtra. Reeling with exhaustion, she had asked for a cup of tea. This simple request threw the entire village into a tizzy. Most people did not know how to make tea, and the ones who did had neither tea leaves nor sugar or milk. Godavari smiled as she remembered how someone had rushed off to get tea leaves from the neighbouring village three kilometres away, while another had managed to produce some jaggery and a third had sent his son to bring back the only nanny goat in the pada from the grazing ground to milk her. A cup of tea, something she had always taken for granted, took three hours to make that day.

She remembered, too, the day she had walked into Mangalpada, caked in dust, and discovered that there was no water to wash herself with until a local Warli woman filled a pot with some water from an algae-infested pond. Shuddering, Godavari recalled how she had been forced to use the same water for drinking. There had been many days like that—of drinking unclean water, trudging through dense jungle, sleeping out in the open and managing without fresh clothes (or tea), often for long stretches of time. This was not the life a privileged upbringing had prepared her for. Yet, she had remained steadfast, committed to her crusade to win justice for the tribals.

And it had not been in vain. She thought back to her first victory in the village of Talasari.

---

36 Parulekar, p. 5.

Having gathered the Adivasis together in a hut, Shamrao and she had spoken at length, trying to unite the tribals in a strike against the landlords. She remembered how she had stood against the backdrop of a red flag pinned to the hut's wall with thorns, how the Warlis had reacted with silence to what was being said. How the local talathi, a minor government official, had swaggered in, accompanied by two of the local landlord's musclemen brandishing clubs. The three had positioned themselves in front of her and gestured menacingly, challenging her to continue speaking.

What happened after that is the stuff local legends are made of. Godavari had looked the talathi square in the eye and demanded that he show her proof of permission for attending a private meeting. She threatened to sue him in court for infringing on her right to speak and for attempting to participate in a private gathering without an official permit. Then she had turned to the musclemen, her eyes narrowed. 'Have you come to scare us or are you scared of us?' she asked loudly. 'Why have you brought these clubs? The days of threatening people with clubs are gone.'

Surprised by this unexpected onslaught, the talathi and his hounds backed down. As they left, the Warlis began to mutter. They had seen it was possible to stand up to the landlords and their henchmen.[37]

What followed was two years of struggle. Godavari had moved from village to village, organising the tribals and teaching them to resist the landlords. Encouraged by the Communist Party, the Warlis refused to act as bonded labourers and demanded fair wages for work done. They endured beatings and whippings, went hungry and were thrown into jail but did not yield. Godavari and Shamrao

---

37 Parulekar, pp. 21–22.

made the red flag and fear of it all-pervasive, and ensured no tribal tolerated any injustice silently. Thousands went to jail.

On 15 August 1947, the jailed tribals went on a hunger strike, stating that they were neither thieves nor criminals and would not celebrate the departure of the British till they too were given freedom. The tide turned, and the Adivasis slowly but steadily won for themselves justice and, most importantly, dignity and respect.

For their role in organising the tribals, the British branded the Parulekar couple as terrorists and sentenced them to long prison terms.[38] Independence did not change their fortunes. The government of the province of Bombay, under the administration of Morarji Desai, who was known for his antipathy towards communists, showed no interest in releasing them. However, the rule of law finally prevailed and they could return home, free again.

As she finished addressing the rally and stepped down from the stage, Godavari did not know that her struggle was far from over. She had fought and won against the British government which, though oppressive and cruel, appeared to believe in some semblance of justice. She would soon have to wage war against a power that was many times more repressive than the one she had fought.

The battle began anew when Godavari embarked on a tour of Dahanu and Umbergaon after her release from jail in 1953. The visit had to be kept secret since she was not permitted to enter these regions as per the terms of her discharge. The tribals greeted her enthusiastically everywhere; their morale was at an all-time high with her amongst them. Fearing she would get lost in the jungles, they walked with her, showing her secret paths she would never have found herself.

---

38   Ibid.

Ankalas, her last stop, was at the edge of the jungle. Beyond it lay a thicket of toddy trees where she would have been completely exposed. They were all aware by now that she was in danger of being discovered. Apparently, some toddy trappers had recognised her and squealed to the police.

The tribals advised Godavari to cross the border into Portuguese territory to escape arrest. To do so, she dressed in a black saree draped Gujarati style, her face covered with the pallu. An old Warli man walked behind her with her clothes, now tied up in a bundle. Whenever they met someone, he would tell them his daughter-in-law was returning from her mother's place. In this way, she reached the Daman Ganga River and the village of Borlai in Nagar Haveli, where more than a dozen village chiefs awaited her. From them, she learnt about the dismal conditions of the tribals in Nagar Haveli. Later, on her journey back to Bombay, she came to the conclusion that these people needed her as much as the Adivasis on the Indian side.

As she set about organising the tribals, Godavari was unaware that events had taken place in Mumbai in 1948 which would present her with a powerful ally for her cause. George Vaz had just parted ways with the Indian National Congress to form the socialist Goa Congress, which would later become the Goan People's Party.

Vaz had initially been a member of the National Congress (Goa), which was aligned with the Indian National Congress. Once a believer in the Gandhian concept of satyagraha, he had become disillusioned after coming in contact with Ram Manohar Lohia and seeing the terror inflicted upon the satyagrahis, gradually began to tread a more militant path. The final break occurred in Bombay when the Indian National Congress organised a meeting on 14 August 1948 to celebrate a year of India's independence. Vaz and his friends protested the meeting. With so many of their allies in jail in Portugal or Goa, the Congress had no cause to celebrate, they said. But the Congress paid no heed to their displeasure, so Vaz, with twenty others, put together the Goan People's Party and allied with Godavari and her tribal followers.[39]

The foundation had been laid for the third and final team.

---

39 Parulekar, pp. 44–144.

Preparations

IT was the beginning of June 1954. Sudhir and Lalita Phadke had just shifted base to Bombay with Shreedhar, their four-year-old son.

Phadke had always been keen on making a career in music. He spent many years travelling all over the country, singing in small mehfils and barely managing to eke out a living. His first significant break came in 1939 when he composed a song that was recorded by HMV, a music company set up in 1908 and, by that time, a force to reckon with in the music industry. Those were the days in which music was recorded on a wax plate, then transferred to a factory in Calcutta, cast onto a metal plate, and sent for approval to the recording studio. If it was approved, HMV made copies for the market.

It took three months for the process to be completed, but Phadke's first recorded song became an instant hit. He went on to compose and sing songs for Marathi and Hindi films, and is best known for his collaborative work with the poet Gajanan Madgulkar, with whom he created the *Geet*

Ramayana,[40] a set of fifty-six songs that tell the story of the Ramayana. The songs were written by Madgulkar and set to music and sung by Phadke as well as many noted singers, including Vasantrao Deshpande, Lata Mangeshkar and Ram Phatak. All India Radio regularly broadcast these tracks and when performed live, they drew packed houses.

Phadke and Lalita Deulikar, who was also a singer, married in 1949. They say Mohammed Rafi sang the mangalashtaka (a set of eight auspicious verses) at the wedding. By the time the couple moved to Bombay, Phadke had started work at Prabhat Film Company, founded by V. Shantaram, as a music director.[41]

The shift to Bombay (now Mumbai) was because it offered better career opportunities in the Hindi film industry. However, the Phadkes kept their Pune bungalow and did not immediately buy a house in Bombay. Instead, they lived in a tiny three-room apartment lent to them by Baburao Pathak, a close friend.

One morning, a middle-aged man walked into this house with a team of ten young men in tow, all carrying small cloth bags. After they had freshened up, changed and had the tea that Lalita offered them, the men (none of whom Lalita recognised) trooped into the inner room.

The Phadkes kept an open house. It was customary to have friends dropping in for mehfils till late at night. Lalita had

---

40   All songs of the *Geet Ramayana* were set to tune with Indian classical music as a base. A new song was broadcast every Friday morning and repeated over the following two days. This was four years before television was introduced and when radio was the prime source of entertainment.

41   Sudhir Phadke, *Jagachya Pathivar*, Rajhans Prakashan, Pune, 2003, pp. 182–189.

always been a part of such sessions, but what had happened that day was unusual—the men gathered in the inner room and Phadke shut the door behind them. All Lalita could hear from inside were whispers.

Her surprise turned to complete bewilderment when Shreedhar ran to her and said, 'Aai, bend down. I have to tell you something.'

She obliged him.

'Aai,' he whispered, 'one of the uncles has a pistol. When he removed his towel, it fell out of his bag.'

Lalita tried to allay her son's fears by telling him it was probably a toy, but he remained unconvinced. He insisted that it had made a solid thud when it fell on the floor, quite unlike one of his toy pistols. She sent him out to play, checked the bags the men had left lined up against the wall and discovered that not one but three of her guests had pistols in their bags.[42]

Many other strange things had begun to happen lately, and they crowded into her mind now.

For one, the number of telephone calls Phadke received had increased, especially late in the evening. As they had no telephone at home, the calls were received by Dr Noman, a physician who had a clinic in the building next-door. His nurse would arrive to alert them to the call, and Phadke would leave anything he was doing to rush and take it. His behaviour was so unusual that the doctor, also a close friend, enquired with genuine concern if all was well. He wondered why Phadke sent everyone out while answering the phone and why he seemed so animated while talking into the receiver. Lalita had no answer to offer the doctor—her husband, who always told her about the events of his day, ignored her questions.

---

42 Phadke, pp. 218–220.

But that day, Lalita was determined to have it out with him.

'Why are these people coming to our house with pistols in their bags?' she demanded. The truth finally tumbled out. The plan for the liberation of Dadra and Nagar Haveli, often discussed in their Pune house, was being executed. An armed assault was to occur, and the young men with pistols were members of the Azad Gomantak Dal. The Dal had decided to join hands with volunteers from the RSS to carry out the operation. Phadke represented the RSS volunteers and Appa Karmalkar, the middle-aged man who led the group, spoke for the Dal. He was here that day to introduce his core team to Phadke.[43]

She asked him then whether his recent two-day trip to Vapi,[44] about which he had told her nothing despite her persistent questioning, was also connected to the plan, and he replied in the affirmative. Her curiosity satisfied, Lalita extracted a promise from her husband that he would take her along whenever he visited Vapi next. His argument about it being possibly dangerous and physically taxing fell on deaf ears. And so, the mission got its first female volunteer, who would soon become one of its most significant assets.

Several meetings were held over the next few weeks, although the venue changed often—usually, they met in public places where strategies were debated and responsibilities assigned. The final meeting was held near Flora Fountain in Bombay.[45]

---

43   Ibid.
44   Vapi is now a booming industrial town and continues to be the closest station to Dadra and Nagar Haveli.
45   Joshi, p. 50.

At this meeting, it was decided that the Azad Gomantak Dal would host training camps and prepare volunteers for the final armed assault. Meanwhile, the RSS volunteers would survey the occupied territories and prepare reports on the placement of the Portuguese police forces, their arms, the locations of the police posts and the possible routes to take. Using this information, they would draft detailed on-the-ground plans. The two groups would jointly establish contact with the locals and establish a support base. They would, of course, unite for the final assault.

The Azad Gomantak Dal had the advantage of knowing the terrain near the border where they could organise camps. They also had a few members who had prior experience in handling weapons. But they didn't have the numbers. Their cadre was scattered, and most of those in India had warrants of arrest against them in Goa. If arrested, they ran the risk of being deported to Goa or some African penal colony.

The RSS, on the other hand, offered a committed cadre and leadership, but had no weapons training or experience in combat.

The overarching worry was that neither group had the funds required for such an ambitious operation. But while the Pune volunteers were still clueless over how to raise funds for arms and training, the Dal had formulated a plan.

Fundraising

THE Azad Gomantak Dal had realised very early on that enthusiasm and good intentions were no substitutes for arms and training, both of which required large sums of money.

In an earlier attempt to raise funds, they had, in 1947, under Vishwanath Lawande and Prabhakar Sinari, attempted to rob the Fazenda in Mapusa. A guard was killed during the raid, and the police arrested Sinari on grounds of suspicion.[46] He was released eventually for lack of proof, after which he promptly teamed up with Lawande once more to rob the Banco Nacional Ultramarino, the bank that handled all financial transactions for the Portuguese in their colonies worldwide.

Although daring, neither attempt resulted in funds accruing to the Dal. In the case of the Fazenda, they could only lay their hands on some cheques since the treasury

---

46   Sinari, p. 47.

officer had transferred the cash to the central treasury just the previous day.

In the case of the bank, they had attempted to snatch the cash while it was being taken from the Mapusa branch to the head office at Panaji. Sinari and two others boarded the public bus and identified the two bank officers who were seated with the bag. They planned to signal their team members, who were standing in wait on the road between Mapusa and Panjim. These men would then stop the bus, board it and make away with the money. However, when Sinari dropped a white handkerchief from the bus window to signal his teammates, one of the bank officers became suspicious. He asked the driver to speed up and pushed the bag under the seat. Sinari managed to grab the bag that he saw in the officer's hand, but it turned out to contain cheques and documents that were of no use to anybody else. Sinari and the two men with him were arrested, and Lawande had to flee to India.[47]

When Sinari met the members of the Dal at its temporary headquarters in 1952 at Belgaum, he found a dispirited lot. His presence was good for their morale, but they still had to find ways to raise money for the struggle ahead. Just then, quite unexpectedly, an opportunity came their way.

The borders of Goa and India were heavily forested and, therefore, porous. Smuggling was rampant. Armaments (readily available in Goa) and gold (which was cheaper) were regularly smuggled into India.

The Customs office in Belgaum, headed by Deputy Superintendent A.S. Dabir, was tasked with preventing the illegal trade. Dalbir knew about the Dal's work and approached them in December 1952. When Lawande and

---

47 Sinari, pp. 47–50.

Dr Jambawalikar, another associate, met Dabir at his official residence, he made them an offer they could not refuse.

'Use your network to provide us with information about the movement of smugglers. In return, we will reward you for seizures made based on your information,' he told them. 'I profoundly appreciate your work,' he added, 'so I will also donate whatever reward money I get for the seizures to the Dal.'[48]

They signed an informal agreement, and the scheme took off. Both sides thrived from the arrangement. The Dal volunteers did all they could to acquire information and track smuggling routes, advising Dabir on where to set up ambush points. He, in turn, always took their tips seriously and mobilised his men, often leading them into the dense forests himself and dealing a devastating blow to smuggling operations, while significantly adding to the Dal's coffers.[49]

As smuggling died down, so did the revenue, but another opportunity presented itself around the beginning of 1953.

The Portuguese government had, at the end of 1952, planned extensive festivities to mark the 400th anniversary of St Xavier's death. Expecting many pilgrims to make the trip, they had also called in soldiers from their African colonies to maintain law and order. The administration now needed large quantities of meat to feed these men and was prepared to pay exorbitant prices. As a result, cattle smuggling became very lucrative. Large herds of cows and buffaloes, even lactating animals, were driven across the border and slaughtered in the jungles. The meat was sold to the Portuguese, although the law expressly prohibited the slaughter of milch cattle.

---

48   Vishvanath Lawande, *Na Ghetale He Vrataandhatene*, p. 147.
49   Lawande, p. 149.

In mid-1953, Azad Gomantak Dal volunteers targeted this illegal trade in cattle. They activated the border police, residents on both sides of the border, as well as social organisations, and carried out raids on cattle smugglers. The rewards added nicely to its coffers.[50] The volunteers in Pune, meanwhile, were at their wit's end as they had no access to assets nor any idea of where to get them from.

Pune, 1954

Rajabhau Wakankar sat with his closest associates, Sudhir Phadke, Moreshwar Purandare and Nana Kajrekar, trying to understand what they needed to do to take the struggle forward.

Moreshwar Purandare, the historian in the group, was a devotee of Chhatrapati Shivaji Maharaja, the legendary Maratha king. He argued that the only way to beat the stronger Portuguese was to use guerrilla warfare. 'Ganimi kava helped the Marathas fight the mighty Mughals for years. It is our only option if we are to beat them,' he insisted.[51]

Huddled together in Phadke's house, the men made a list of things they still had to do. There were weapons to procure and volunteers to enroll and train. It was also important to establish a local support network. After all, guerrilla warfare would be impossible without a deep understanding of the numerically superior enemy's strengths and choke points. They knew it could all be done, but the mood was pensive— they urgently needed money.

Nobody had surplus personal funds they could contribute to the operation—they all worked day jobs that provided just enough for them to scrape by. They came from lower-

---

50 Lawande, p. 150–155.

51 In conversation with B.M. Purandare, historian.

middle-class families with minimal assets. The only one amongst them with a proper career was Phadke. However, while he had done commendable work as an upcoming music director, he was riddled with debts from his early days of struggle. Their sole pistol and rifle were on loan from an ex-army friend, and they could expect nothing more from their existing sources. Moreover, whatever money they had raised had been spent on the first few trips. Funds would have to come from elsewhere now.[52]

Launching a collection drive amongst relatives and friends was briefly considered and rejected—it would mean discussing plans with too many people, which might compromise the secrecy of the operation. One single leak would alert the Portuguese as well as the Indian government, which would uphold the 'liberation of Goa only by the Goans' policy enunciated by Nehru and pack them off to jail.

Contacting prominent individuals was an option, but they knew it could only go the Goa Vimochan Sahayak Samiti way.

The Goa Vimochan Sahayak Samiti, or committee for aiding the Goan liberation, had started operations in late 1953. Based in Pune, it was supported by the Indian National Congress and the left-leaning Praja Socialist Party, which took inspiration from Ram Manohar Lohia. Its volunteers regularly staged peaceful protests on the border of Goa. They had even attempted to cross the border, only to be brutally assaulted and pushed back.

Wakankar had approached Jayantrao Tilak,[53] grandson of the legendary firebrand leader Lokmanya Tilak and one of

---

52   Joshi, p. 53.

53   The Marathi newspaper *Kesari* started by Lokmanya Tilak in 1881 is still published online and edited by his great-grandson Deepak Tilak.

the founders of the Vimochan Sahayak Samiti, for support. After lengthy discussions with him and the other founders, Keshavrao Jedhe and N.G. Gore, Wakankar was told that the Samiti would consider extending support if the men could convince them of their genuineness. Since the group only had a rifle and pistol, they borrowed some weapons from sympathisers in the police and invited Tilak to see them. As a precaution, they blindfolded him and took him to the hideout in a borrowed vehicle. The result? Complete silence and no help. Whether the reason was the Samiti's commitment to non-violence or whether it was the left-leaning Praja Socialist Party's antipathy to the RSS was something the group never understood. Finally, however, they realised that external aid was not an option.[54]

That was when music came to their rescue. Wakankar suggested that Phadke organise a musical programme to raise money since he was known as an upcoming music director. He wouldn't be able to draw a crowd on his own, so they considered the names of C. Ramchandra, the renowned music director and Pannalal Ghosh, the flautist, but Phadke rejected both.

'We need someone who can attract huge crowds,' he said. 'Let's talk to Lata didi.'[55]

Those were the days of Indian cinema when melody was king and Lata Mangeshkar the queen. The oldest daughter of Deenanath Mangeshkar, she was born in 1929 in Sangli, a small town in Maharashtra, into a house filled with music.

---

54 Joshi, p. 53.
55 Ibid.

Her father was a reputed classical vocalist and a leading star of Marathi theatre. He specialised in the sangeet natak genre, where all the leading actors sang semi-classical compositions live as part of the play. Despite his pre-eminence, he was heavily mired in debt and when he died in 1942, the responsibility of supporting the family fell upon the thirteen-year-old Lata. She sang her first song for the Marathi movie *Kitee Hasaal* the same year. Though the song did not make it past the editorial stage, her career took off and she began singing for numerous Hindi and Marathi movies. Her breakthrough came when her song *Uthaye Ja Unke Sitam* in *Andaz* (1949) became a hit. Her songs for *Barsaat* under the music direction of Shankar Jaikishen also became hits and sealed a lifelong partnership between them. The partnership blossomed with films such as *Aah, Daag* and *Awaraa*. If the songs of *Anarkali* and *Do Bigha Zameen* established her superstardom, her song *Jadugar Saiyan Chhod Mori Baiyan* for the film *Nagin*, released in March 1954, sealed her cult-like status. When she sang at concerts, the tickets sold out within hours.

Lata had just shifted into her flat in Walkeshwar when Phadke and his friends met her. Phadke had not only been her music director for a few early Marathi movies but had also sung with her. While the others thought such an acquaintance was enough to persuade her to sing for them, Phadke knew otherwise. She was always polite and respectful to everyone but kept her feelings to herself—no one ever knew what she was thinking. He knew she would hear them out and either agree instantly or refuse point-blank, but whatever it was, once she had decided, no one could persuade her to act otherwise.[56]

---

56 Nasreen Munni Kabir, *Lata Mangeshkar in Her Own Voice*, Niyogi Books, New Delhi, 2009, p. 29–49.

She was hesitant when Phadke told her they had come to request her to sing at a concert to raise funds for a worthy cause. While she heard him out patiently, he could see she was unconvinced. She assured them that she would consider it and get back in touch, and was about to move away when, in desperation, Phadke started telling her about the actual plan. The passion with which he spoke probably moved her, for when he mentioned that the liberation of Dadra and Nagar Haveli was only a prelude to the freedom of Goa, her eyes suddenly welled up with tears.

What Phadke and the others did not know then was the depth of her emotional connection to Goa. Lord Mangesh, or Shiva, in the temple in the village of Mangeshi in north Goa, was her family's presiding deity. The family derived their surname from the name of the village. The Portuguese had been regularly harassing devotees who came to the temple, and the frustration of not being able to do anything about that brought her over to their side in an instant.

'You will allow me to serve my Lord Mangesh,' she said tearfully. 'I wish I could come and fight by your side, but since I cannot, I will help you raise resources. You tell me the date and I will be there.'[57]

The jubilation at securing her assent doubled when she suggested they invite Mohammed Rafi to sing with her. Before they left her place, she rang Rafi to tell him they were coming to see him.

Born in 1924, Rafi was slightly older than Lata and had carved out a unique place for himself in the Indian film and

---

57   Joshi, p. 53.

music industry. If there was a romantic duet to be sung in a Hindi film, Lata and Rafi would sing it. Lata respected him greatly and always referred to him as Rafi Sahab.

When she told him she was singing for a worthy cause and invited him to join her, Rafi readily said yes.

He met them at the newly inaugurated Mehboob Studios in Bandra. When Phadke, with whom Rafi was on excellent terms, explained their mission, all he wanted to know from them was the where and when. A meeting that was supposed to have lasted for ten minutes went on for a full hour as Rafi asked question after question about how they were planning to execute their plans. He was so impressed that he held up a hand when Nana Kajrekar told him he would arrange his railway tickets to and from Pune.

'This country is also mine,' Rafi said, 'and if all of you are preparing to put your lives on the line for it, the least I can do is buy my tickets.'

Rafi inadvertently made another significant contribution. During the conversation, he asked Phadke what his answer would be if someone were to ask why the programme was taking place. After all, a reason was required while seeking permission from the authorities to conduct an event. When Phadke looked blank, Rafi himself provided the answer.

'Bata do ki Shreedhar ka birthday hai,' he said.[58]

This suggestion came in handy while applying for mandatory municipal and police approvals. All the documentation for the program mentioned Shreedhar's birthday as the reason for the concert.

---

58   Nana Kajrekar, *Smarangatha*, Dadra Nagar Haveli Swatantrata Sangram Charitable Society, Pune, 1994, p. 46.

The team also contacted C. Ramchandra, who readily agreed to join them. So the group left Mumbai in very high spirits. Now all they had to do was organise the concert.

Hectic parlays began even as the group returned to Pune.

The first thing they had to decide was, of course, the venue. Since the concert would require a large open space in the central part of the city for easy accessibility, there was only one choice, really: the Deccan Club grounds in Hirabaug.

But when they walked into the club to make a booking for the grounds, Phadke and Wakankar found it the centre of frenetic activity. People were rushing about erecting tents, building a stage, arranging chairs—Prithvi Theatres had already booked the venue! They found out that the Bombay-based theatre company founded by Prithviraj Kapoor was organising a theatre festival, with performances slated to be held every night through April.

As they turned despondently to exit the club, mulling over the problem of finding another equally good venue, they ran into Vasant Zanzale, who was responsible for the arrangements on the ground. He knew Phadke well and was also a fan of Wakanker's kabaddi-playing prowess. When they explained their problem, he gave them the solution. One of the theatre companies had cancelled its participation, so the facilities would free between 18 and 20 April—the same days they were thinking of!

Zanzale offered to talk to the manager of Prithvi Theatres and Prithviraj Kapoor to let them use it on the required dates. He was sure they would not deny a Lata–Rafi show some space. And indeed, they did not. Zanzale quickly obtained the permits and waived the rent of the tent and accessories, asking them to pay only the operating expenses, and that too only after they had sold the tickets. Zanzale's involvement did not end here—he would join them at the time of the final assault on Silvassa.

Preparations began in earnest, and the group released a few advertisements in local dailies, including *Kesari*. Not having the funds for extensive advertising, they resorted to unconventional ways of spreading the word about the programme. Volunteers launched a word-of-mouth campaign, went to busy intersections early in the morning and wrote with white paint on tar roads advertising the program. The result was that all the tickets were sold out.[59]

Everything was set for the musical night. People streamed in on the appointed day and packed the tent to the brim. But as the orchestra played popular tunes to keep the audience engaged, bad news arrived: Lata Mangeshkar's car had met with an accident on the narrow, hilly roads between Pune and Bombay.

While navigating the hairpin bends on the highway, her driver had dozed off and collided with a tractor on the opposite side. Though she was not seriously hurt, the police escorted her back to her residence and called to say she could not make it.[60]

Phadke was stunned. Their plan had come undone in one unexpected stroke. While the long-term implications were huge, the immediate repercussions had to be handled first. The crowd had gathered to listen to Lata and Rafi, and had been making do with an orchestra until now. But people were fidgeting, moving about and beginning to murmur. How the

---

59   Joshi, p. 55.
60   Ibid.

restive crowd would behave if Lata and Rafi did not appear on stage soon was anybody's guess.

The team debated the right way of communicating the news to the audience. Some suggested that other singers, including Phadke, begin the programme and settle the crowd, following which someone could announce the accident.

Phadke and Wakankar, after some thought, turned down the suggestion. They preferred to be upfront and tell the audience about it right away. 'I am a performing artist,' Phakde said, 'the audience is my godhead. I cannot lie to them.'

Announcing the cancellation was fraught with risk since a similar last-minute cancellation announcement in Nagpur a few months before had resulted in a near riot-like situation. The angry crowd had upturned the furniture, burnt the tent and beaten up the organisers.

Nevertheless, both men insisted on being straightforward with the audience, and Phadke stepped up on stage. There was pin-drop silence when he began speaking. 'Lata-ji has met with an accident,' he told the audience. 'We could have continued the programme and announced this halfway, but we preferred to share it with you immediately.'[61]

He added that the programme stood cancelled but would be rescheduled at the same venue soon, and the dates would be announced based on Lata's health. He asked those wanting a refund to claim it from the ticket counter. Such was his reputation in Pune, and so apparent was his sincerity that very few asked for a refund. However, those who wanted it got it immediately. Phadke's candour had thankfully averted an ugly incident.[62]

---

61   In conversation with Shreedhar Phadke.
62   Joshi, p. 55.

Meanwhile, Lata realised she was not seriously hurt except for a gash on her forehead. Once it was patched up, she arranged for a car and left once more for Pune with Rafi. She called Phadke before leaving, but no one took the call as everyone was at the concert venue. Lata then called Bhalji Pendharkar, a reputed Marathi film producer known to both her and Phadke, and asked him to communicate the message. He was then in Kolhapur and rang a friend in Pune, who rushed to the venue with the information that Lata and Rafi were on the way. Unfortunately, by then, the damage had already been done. Phadke had announced the cancellation, and the crowds had dispersed.

Lata and Rafi finally arrived at the venue at 11.30 p.m. and saw that it was dark and deserted. The incident in Nagpur still fresh in her mind, and worried about Phadke's safety, she rushed to his house. Alighting from the car, she ran up the stairs and barged into his drawing room. When she saw that Phadke was safe, she fainted and had to be taken to a doctor.[63]

She stayed with the Phadkes that night and, before leaving, promised that she would cancel whatever she was doing to perform on whichever date they scheduled the concert for next.

The concert was finally held on 2 May at the same venue. Zanzale had not dismantled the tented auditorium after the theatre festival ended and permitted its use. The programme was a hit, and though the venue was not as jam-packed with listeners as the first time, the revenue was still substantial.[64]

Lata Mangeshkar's parting words were a huge morale booster for the group.

---

63   Joshi, p. 56.
64   Ibid.

'You are going to win,' she said as she got into her car for the drive back to Bombay. 'Until you do and liberate my Mangeshi temple, I will be with you in spirit every step of the way. Whenever you need my help, you must call me.'[65]

It was a good beginning, and their confidence was high.

---

65   Joshi, p. 53.

Under the Table

IT was February 1948, and India and Pakistan had been independent for six months. Besides Hyderabad, every other princely state had formally acceded to either of the two countries. The Nizam of Hyderabad, confident of British support and with the tacit backing of Pakistan, had decided that his kingdom would remain independent.

On 27 November 1947, the Nizam signed a standstill agreement with India[66] by which both sides agreed to maintain the status quo for a year, i.e., till the end of November 1948.[67] The Nizam used this period to petition the British for aid, negotiate with Pakistan, and take the matter to the United Nations (UN).

Meanwhile, the internal situation in Hyderabad was going from bad to worse. The Arya Samaj and the Congress

---

66   Mohammed Hyder, *October Coup: A Memoir of the Struggle for Hyderabad*, Roli Books, New Delhi, 2012, p. 8.

67   Syed Ali Hashmi, *Hyderabad 1948: An Avoidable Invasion*, Pharos Media and Publishing, New Delhi, 2017, p. 114.

organised peaceful protests, while communist groups in the Telengana region took up arms against the feudatories of the Nizam. The Indian Army was exerting pressure too, and an armed invasion loomed on the horizon.

The Nizam's appeals to the British went unheeded. They responded to his letters, but only with platitudes. His faith in Pakistan and the UN remained unshaken though, based on which he decided to order his forces to resist any Indian intervention. He was convinced that if his troops could hold out for a week or so against the Indian Army, he could draw international attention to the situation and turn the tide to Hyderabad's advantage.

Resisting the Indian forces was easier said than done, as the Nizam's army had only 6,000 fully trained soldiers and some 18,000 irregulars. There was also a grave shortage of arms and ammunition. When the soldiers who had fought alongside the Allies in World War II returned to Hyderabad, the British had retained the machine guns, Bren guns, mortars and other weaponry purchased with Hyderabad's state funds, with the promise of replacements from the Indian armoury. That never happened. Instead, the Indian government initiated an economic blockade that crippled the state.

All attempts at setting up arms manufacturing units within Hyderabad were unsuccessful because the necessary machinery could not be imported. The Nizam's army then tried to produce rifles by converting the railway repair workshops into gun manufacturing factories, but the rifles they manufactured were substandard and often exploded in the hands of the soldiers.

Initially, the answer to the staffing crisis seemed to lie in the Razakars, the voluntary militant wing of the Majlis-E-Ittehadul Muslimeen, led by Kasim Rizvi. Rizvi boasted that over five lakh Razakars would take to the streets if India invaded Hyderabad.[68] The statement, of course, was more bluster than substance, but it did raise fears of communal riots and violence against the minority Hindu population should the Indian Army cross the border into Hyderabad.

It was at this fragile time that Fredrick Sidney Cotton met the Nizam with an alluring offer.

Cotton was an Australian aviator who had flown for the Royal Air Force (RAF) during World War II. He was known to be a great personal friend of Winston Churchill and Ian Fleming. It was even rumoured that Fleming had modelled James Bond, at least partly, on him.

After World War II came to an end, Cotton started trading in surplus wartime supplies, which he resold at enormous profits. He had just arrived in Calcutta to collect some equipment when he heard about the economic blockade of Hyderabad. Sensing an opportunity, he made his way to the city and met the prime minister, Mir Laiq Ali, with an offer to fly out the groundnut crop that was one of Hyderabad's principal exports, and of which huge stocks lay rotting due to the blockade.[69]

During the meeting, the discussion veered to the critical state of the economy due to the blockade. Cotton expressed indignation at India's 'bullying' and suggested that if the Nizam arranged the purchase of weapons, he would smuggle them into Hyderabad via Pakistan.

The plan was simple: he would pick up the arms from Karachi, overfly Indian territory at night and deliver them to an airport near Hyderabad. He was confident that he would not be stopped as his Lockheed was superior to the Hawker Tempests, Hurricanes and Spitfires that the Indian Air Force

---

68   Hashmi, p. 49.

69   Hashmi, p. 114.

used. It could fly higher and faster than their planes. Also, he believed the Indian pilots were not trained to carry out night sorties. His proposal was a godsend for the beleaguered prime minister and Syed Ahmed El Edroos, the commander-in-chief of the Hyderabad State Forces.[70]

At the beginning of June 1948, Cotton met the Nizam in his Chowmahalla Palace in the presence of Laiq Ali and El Edroos. The palace, located near the Charminar, was the seat of the Asaf Jahi dynasty. It was built in the late eighteenth century and had two huge courtyards, lawns, fountains and a massive, marble-floored Darbar hall. Cotton admired the opulent beauty of the structure but could not help noticing the thick layer of grime inside the room, which was stuffy and airless with all the curtains drawn. The floor looked as if it had not been scrubbed in years; cigarette butts carpeted the area.

The contrast between the nattily clad Cotton and the Nizam, in his tattered fez and sherwani, was stark.[71] The Nizam came straight to the point. 'I wish to buy weapons to protect my country. I want everything: machine guns, grenades, mortars and anti-aircraft guns. And I want them delivered very soon. You have five weeks to transport them to my country.'

'That is entirely possible, Your Exalted Highness,' Cotton replied. 'However, my fee is twenty million pounds—in cash.'[72]

For the Nizam, this was a small price to pay for his country's freedom. He gave his consent instantly, and a plan was put in

---

70 Omar Khalidi, *Memoirs of Sidney Cotton*, Hyderabad Historical Society, Hyderabad, 1994, p. 30.

71 Jeff Watson, *Sidney Cotton: The Last Plane Out of Berlin*, Hachette, Sydney, 2009, pp. 12–13.

72 Watson, p. 100.

motion. El Edroos placed an order with a Czech company for 500 tonnes of arms and ammunition worth forty million rupees, to be delivered to Switzerland.[73] They would then be moved to Karachi and transported from there to Hyderabad within five weeks. Laiq Ali wrote a letter to Muhammad Ali Jinnah detailing the arrangements and handed it to Cotton. Cotton promised that the entire airlift operation would be completed in three days. Shifting 500 tonnes of armaments within such a short time was close to impossible, but it was the kind of challenge that Cotton enjoyed.

The first obstacle came up at the very beginning when Skyways, the company contracted to fly the weapons to Karachi, backed out, fearing retribution from the government. Since the news had leaked by then, Cotton knew he must hurry or risk being stopped. So he leased ten planes from Skyways and the Irish company Air Lingus and recruited a crew of sixty.[74] They took off from London on 11 May 1948 and, picking up the cargo from Basel in Switzerland, reached Karachi on 13 May. On the way, they had to stop to refuel at Malta, where Cotton's audacity saved the day for them. When asked what they were carrying, he smiled and said, 'We are loaded to the roof with arms and ammunition.' Laughing at what he thought was a joke, the airport official stamped the documents and waved them on.[75]

The first plane, piloted by Cotton, landed at Warangal airport, about fifty kilometres from Hyderabad, on 4 June. El Edroos and Laiq Ali received the consignment with gratitude and gave Cotton a revised target of 3,000 tonnes. He flew sixteen times more to meet the new target, landing mostly

---

73   Ibid.

74   Ibid, p. 115.

75   Ibid, p. 116.

at Bidar airport, 150 kilometres from Hyderabad. Along with arms and ammunition, he smuggled in essential medical supplies and baby food. This was probably to divert attention in case anyone got suspicious.[76] The cover, however, was blown when on one of the last flights scheduled at the end of June, a field gun broke loose during take-off, and the plane became tail-heavy and crashed. The pilot, Jerome Frewin, and three others died, and guns were scattered all over Karachi airport. The news travelled to India, where the press quickly picked it up. The Indian government reacted immediately too. On 25 July, Nehru warned Hyderabad to either accede or prepare for war. The warning was never officially acknowledged, but the Nizam halted the airlifts, so the anti-tank weapons, a later addition to the wish list, never reached Hyderabad.

Cotton, however, had succeeded in his mission. He had transported 1,000 anti-tank mines, 25,000 mortars, 1,200 Biretta submachine guns, 3,000 submachine carbines, 10,000 rifles and a lone ack-ack (anti-aircraft) gun, besides a considerable amount of ammunition.[77]

By now, the Hyderabad State Congress had become more active and were protesting even more vociferously. They were put down with a firm hand and had to shift their base across the border following India's independence. They set up eleven camps in places like Chicholi, Gondgaon and Wagholi. From there, they carried out raids into Hyderabadi territory, and organised dharnas and demonstrations seeking to disrupt the civil administration. There were others with criminal

---

76   Ibid.
77   Ibid, p. 100.

intent, who set up camp in Sundir, Jawali and Upla only to loot and pillage inside Hyderabadi territory. With its meagre resources, the civil administration could not protect the villages on the border and increasingly relied on the Pathans, who were irregular members of the army, and the Razakars,[78] which caused further polarisation. The raiders from the Indian side targeted the Muslims and the Pathans, while the Razakars assaulted the Hindus. Many of the irregulars also ran extortionary protection rackets. Despite all this, as per the standstill agreement, the armies did not deploy in areas within three kilometres of the Indian border.

With Hyderabad refusing to yield, the Indian Army began occupying positions on the border and shut down all the camps by mid-August. The Congress workers were told to tone down their protests as the forces prepared for direct action.[79]

The Nizam, however, seemed confident that India would do nothing until November. A delegation was sent to the UN on 10 September 1948. But then, on 13 September, before the UN could come to a decision, the Indian troops, led by Major General J.N. Chaudhuri, entered Hyderabad. Supported by tanks, the army infiltrated via Osmanabad, Tulzapur, Naldurg and many other vantage points, beating back the demoralised Hyderabadi troops. Resistance, if any, was offered by the Pathans and the Razakars. In a surprising move, the communists who had fought against the Nizam till then, joined hands with the Razakars and were given access to the guns that Cotton had smuggled in. But the battle soon reduced to minor scuffles on the streets between the two sides. As the Indian Army swept aside resistance,

---

78   Hyder, p. 6.
79   Ibid, p. 69.

the skirmishers withdrew into the forests of the Telangana region, from where they ran a parallel government till 1951. The resistance by the communists and the difficulty faced by the Indian government in controlling the insurgency would later play a crucial role in the fight against the Portuguese in Nagar Haveli in 1954.

The government headed by Laiq Ali had been confident of its ability to defend the city. The anti-tank guns which were stuck in Cairo would soon be delivered, it was thought, enabling the state troops to turn the tide. But, in a dramatic development, the prime minister and his cabinet suddenly resigned on the morning of 17 September 1948 and handed over the running of the state to the Nizam.

On the same day, Rizvi went on air on Deccan Radio, apologising to the people of Hyderabad for failing to protect them. Then he had weapons distributed to thousands of his supporters with orders to carry out a genocide of Hindus should the Indian Army enter the city of Hyderabad.[80] However, Mohammad Hyder, a civil servant of Osmanabad, rushed with this news to Nawab Deen Yar Jung, the police chief, who managed to convince Rizvi to withdraw the order.[81]

The Indian forces swept through the territories of the Nizam and entered the capital city on 18 September. The following day, the Nizam asked his commander-in-chief El Edroos whether he could defend the city for three days.

'Not even three hours, Your Exalted Highness,' he replied. He signed an unconditional surrender on the same day, and Hyderabad ceased to be under the Nizam's control.[82]

---

80   Ibid, p. 76.
81   Ibid, p. 77.
82   Ibid, p. 78.

The Nizam was allowed to retain his palaces and properties and was appointed the titular head of Hyderabad state as the Raj Pramukh or governor. Laiq Ali fled to Pakistan, while, while Rizvi was arrested and handed over to the Indian Army. The Pakistani government, meanwhile, denied payments to Sydney Cotton for his services and he retired to live out the rest of his life in poverty.

The Indian Army seized large caches of arms, but many of the Razakars retreated to the villages, taking their weapons with them. For many years afterwards, Hyderabad remained the central hub of the black market in arms and ammunition, where anyone with the right contacts could buy guns at very reasonable prices.

It was this market that the Pune team, led by Raja Wakankar, targeted in the beginning of 1954.

Lock and Load

ALTHOUGH the rescheduled concert of Lata Mangeshkar and Mohammed Rafi was a success, the audience had been smaller than the first time. Roughly ₹10,000 remained after all the expenses had been taken care of. A small amount was squirrelled away for emergencies. What was left for the purchase of arms was, therefore, much lesser than expected.

While their resources were limited, the group's ambitions were not. They planned to arm twenty or more volunteers who would help capture police outposts in the territories surrounding Silvassa before joining up with the Azad Gomantak Dal volunteers to attack town and liberate it. After that, they planned to take Daman, and then Goa.[83]

Everything hinged on first securing Dadra and Nagar Haveli. For this, they needed more weapons. Wakankar, Phadke, Shantaram Vaidya and Parshuram Sane came

---

83   B.M. Purandare, Smruti Visheshank, *Dadra Nagar Haveli Mukti Sangram Samiti*, Pune, 2004, p. 55.

together to figure out a way forward. The tall and athletic Vaidya was an ace marksman who had won plaudits for his marksmanship during a stint with the National Cadet Corps while in college, and was the most adept at handling firearms.[84] Sane had extensive contacts among the veterans in his hometown Junnar, who could be of help in training volunteers. Sane also had a close friend who knew how to fix defective weapons.[85]

After taking stock of the situation, the group decided to source weapons from Hyderabad, from the cache originally delivered to the Nizam by Sydney Cotton.

During the first week of July 1954, Wakankar, Kajrekar and Sane reached Hyderabad by train. Purshottam Badwe, who had arrived a day in advance to mobilise his network, met them at the station. A wrestler who regularly took part in tournaments, Badwe often travelled to Hyderabad from his hometown Pandharpur, which was close to the old Hyderabad border. He had offered to activate his wrestling contacts to connect them to the black market, and sure enough, he had come up with a name and a place—Mohammad Wahab and the Golconda Fort.[86]

The Golconda Fort, built by the Kakatiyas in 1143, had originally been a mud fort which got its name from the granite hill, Golli Konda, on which it was built. The Bahmani kings added to it, while the Qutub Shahi dynasty, in the fifteenth century, demolished the mud walls and erected granite ones. Rising 130 meters above the ground, the fort was long considered to be impregnable. Due to its proximity

---

84　Handwritten notes by Shantaram Vaidya, sourced from his son Captain Sanjay Vaidya.

85　Purandare, Visheshank, p. 41.

86　In conversation with B.M. Purandare, historian.

to the famed Kollur Mine, which was the source of the Nizam's fabulous wealth as well as the only known source of diamonds in the world during the 17th century, it soon became a flourishing centre of trade.

In 1687, Emperor Aurangzeb captured and ransacked the fort after a protracted eight-month-long siege, leaving it in ruins. Over the next few decades, as the Mughal empire became weaker, their viceroy in the Deccan, Mir Qamar-ud-din Khan Siddiqi, seized power. In 1724, he declared himself independent and began to rule, as Asif Jah I, from Aurangabad. In 1769, his grandson, Asif Jah III, moved the capital from Aurangabad to Hyderabad, where it remained till the state, under Asif Jah VII, the last Nizam, acceded to India in 1948.

Despite the diamond mines, Golconda Fort never regained its former grandeur, and the village at its base shrank to a handful of houses. Wahab was a resident of this village and acted as a tourist guide for the occasional visitor. Badwe's contact had told him that Wahab knew of a cache of arms that was up for sale. The source also endorsed him as a reliable person in a market rife with cheats and ruffians where suppliers could disappear after taking money, or even turn violent.

Wahab met the team near the Dargah opposite the Golconda fort. A tall, thin man who walked with a slight stoop, he told them he had never been a Razakar. However, when his Razakar friends returned to the village with their weapons, he had suggested a place where they could be stashed. When subsequent searches by the Indian Army failed to unearth them, others started asking for their arms to be stowed there too. Soon, Wahab had accumulated a substantial cache of rifles, pistols and ammunition—even a light machine gun.[87]

---

87   In conversation with B.M. Purandare, historian.

He told them now that the hiding place was just a kilometre away, and they followed him in the pitch dark, increasingly nervous. Having already made the payment, they knew they were at his mercy. If he disappeared into the darkness, there was nothing they could do but head back to Pune. Within a few minutes, however, crumbling ramparts of the fort came into view, and then a terrible stench hit them. They later learned that this area was an extension of the Golconda Fort called the Naya Quila. The stench came from the largest rubbish dump in the city, which ran alongside the fort.

Soon enough, they arrived at their destination and realised why the weapons had remained safe all these years—the hiding place was a tree.

It was a baobab, Wahab told them. Brought as a sapling by the Nizam from Madagascar, it was at least four centuries old and was known locally as 'hathiyon ka jhad', or the elephant tree, because of the shape of its branches. The tree trunk, with a circumference of nearly twenty-five metres, made an ideal hiding place.

The light from the mosque behind it lit up parts of the tree, shone through the branches and cast eerie shadows around it. Wahab scampered up the branches and seemed to vanish when he reached the centre. After a while, he emerged with a ladder and asked them to ascend. Wakankar did so, and discovered that the cavity at the centre of the trunk had been fashioned into two rooms, each roughly ten feet in length and breadth. Wahab held up the lantern he was carrying, so Wakankar could see the arsenal scattered across the two rooms. These rooms, Wahab said, had once been the hiding place of a gang of forty thieves.[88] He retrieved the ladder from outside and descended with the first tranche of arms for

---

88   In conversation with B.M. Purandare, historian.

the movement—three rifles.[89] Loading these into a wooden trunk they had carried, the four headed back to the railway station and took the next train to Pune.

~

Kajrekar and Wakankar had just exited the station carrying the wooden box between them when they heard someone yell, 'Thamba!'. They turned to see the on-duty policeman running towards them, gesturing wildly at them to stop and put the box down. They complied, since the box was too heavy to run with and, in any case, doing so would have meant an admission of guilt. They folded their hands and humbly told the policeman that the box only contained some household articles. The constable was stubborn and demanded that they get the contents inspected. He had concluded they were opium smugglers from Hyderabad and sensed an opportunity to make a quick profit. He said he would let the box through only if they paid him ₹400. It was either that or take the box to the police station for a thorough inspection. Naturally, the group preferred the former option. The only issue was that nobody had the money to pay him off.

With a persuasiveness born of desperation, Wakankar convinced the policeman to wait for some time. 'I don't have the money, but I'll wait with you while my friends go and fetch it. We can have a cup of tea together, and when they return, you can let us go.'[90]

The policeman agreed. Wakankar and Sane lifted the box and, crossing the road, placed it outside the teashop by the roadside. While they kept the policeman busy with small talk

---

89 Purandare, Visheshank, p. 42.

90 Joshi, p. 60.

over a cup of tea, the other two carried the box away. And without that, there was nothing the policeman could do. If he still insisted on a bribe, they could raise a hue and cry about corrupt policemen trying to extract money from innocent travellers. He slunk away.[91]

The close shave taught them a lesson—never again would weapons be brought in as one consignment. Instead, they took each weapon apart in Hyderabad, transporting it in separate parts through Jalna, Mumbai and Pune, and reassembling it later in Satara. Children of friends and relatives came to their help when transporting ammo. They would turn up at the train station in Pune in their school uniforms as if to receive relatives, enter the compartments, pocket the bullets, prance out and hand them over after exiting the station.[92] The only problem was the lone Bren gun, which they could not disassemble. So Phadke obtained a violin case from his friend V.G. Jog, a violin player, and stuffed the gun inside. When he got down at the Pune station, he brazenly walked past the police officers on duty. Phadke was known locally as a musician, so they did not harass him. It was such an effective ruse that he carried the violin case with him right up to the day of the assault on Silvassa.[93]

Despite all precautions, there were other near disasters. One occurred when Sham Rao Lad, a volunteer of the Azad Gomantak Dal, procured some explosives from Belgaum. He packed them into small canvas bags and stored these in his house in Bhatewadi, Mumbai. One day, while Phadke, Kajrekar, Lad and Appa Karmalkar were having one of their regular meetings in the front room of his house, tendrils of

---

91   Ibid.

92   Conversation with Vasant Prasade, freedom fighter.

93   Purandare, Visheshank, p. 42.

smoke began rising into the air—one of the bags had caught fire. Within seconds, the house was filled with smoke. Showing admirable presence of mind, Lad swiftly dumped the smouldering bag in a bucket full of water. Had he not done so in time, the explosion would have blown the building to bits.

After the initial transaction, the group made four more trips to the baobab tree and procured six more rifles, three revolvers and one Bren gun.[94] Far from sufficient for the planned attack on the Silvassa police post, but it was something.

The entire cache of arms was then taken to the village of Rethare, near Karhad, approximately 160 kilometres from Pune, and stored on the farm of Sadguru Vishnu Patil, a friend of Sane. There was a small building in the middle of his farm that served as a storage space, a repair workshop and a shooting range. Sane's ex-army friend, Appa, worked here during the day, assembling the weapons, repairing them and getting them battle-ready. Patil himself, a well-educated farmer with a technical bent of mind, would often assist him. Together, they ensured that most of the weapons were serviceable. Even transporting the weapons had its share of near catastrophes. Tasked with carrying a set of pistols to Rethare for repair, Sane nonchalantly put them in a cloth bag and boarded the train for Karad. As he waited for the train to pull out of the station, a group of policemen entered the compartment, crowding him into a corner. Convinced that they had learned about the pistols but not daring to leave the compartment lest it escalate matters, he discreetly pushed the cloth bag under the seat with his foot.

---

94   Ibid.

'Is this compartment reserved for policemen? I can go elsewhere if it is,' he said, with a studied air of deference.

The policeman sitting across from him laughed. 'You keep sitting, bhau. There has been a dacoity at Neera, we are going there to handle the situation. We saw some empty seats on this train, so we got on.'

Sane heaved a sigh of relief, and a posse of police thus unknowingly escorted the illegal consignment of pistols halfway to its storage point.[95]

The group would often retire to Karad and practise using the weapons under the watchful eye of Shantaram Vaidya. When Patil's neighbours asked about the sound of rifles firing at night, he would tell them he was bursting crackers to scare away animals.

To maintain this cover, Patil took to actually bursting crackers, even when the others were not practising. While doing so one day, he made an interesting discovery—he tossed one into an empty tin container in the storeroom and found that the sound matched that of a rifle firing explosively. He immediately demonstrated this to Wakankar and they decided that volunteers would burst crackers in empty tin containers when attacking, in order to give the impression that they had more guns than they possessed and demoralise the Portuguese.[96]

May–July 1954

While the folks from Pune were acquiring and learning how to use weapons, the Azad Gomantak Dal took upon itself the task of training its cadres.

---

95   Parshuram Sane, *Smritigandh*, p. 34.
96   In conversation with Vasant Prasade and Captain Sanjay Vaidya.

The first camp was organised at Amboli in the jungles in India, very close to the Goan border.[97] Fifty volunteers joined the ten-day training programme run by Captain Digambar Gole, a retired army officer.

A World War II veteran with over twenty years of active service, Gole had extensive experience in the handling of explosives, operating and repairing wireless sets and handling small arms. He and his immediate superior, Colonel Sherjung Choudhary, had trained village volunteer forces in Kashmir during the 1947 invasion by Pakistan and had done their job so well that Prime Minister Nehru had personally lauded their efforts.

Mornings at the camp were devoted to learning how to handle explosives, making rope bridges, mountain climbing, etc. The trainees spent the nights crawling through the undergrowth, jumping over obstacles and learning to approach targets undetected. In the absolute darkness of the jungles, they conducted mock raids on police stations and learned how to sharpen their night vision.[98] For an hour every day, Lawande and Lad spoke to them about the history of the movement and its ultimate objectives.

The last two days were the most exciting for the group as they learned how to handle firearms. But it also put them at risk of being discovered by the Indian authorities. Whereas all their other activities could be explained, the unmistakable sound of weapons being fired could not. With Nehru opposing even peaceful satyagraha against the Portuguese on Indian soil, the discovery of an armed camp would have resulted in the immediate arrest of the Dal volunteers.

---

97 Lawande, p. 165.
98 Sinari, p. 108.

In the initial stages, Eknath Joshi, a local Congress activist, kept the police off their backs. But, after the second session, the training shifted to the Goan side of the border. Six such sessions were held, each one with only fifteen trainees, to ensure maximum focus. After accounting for some dropouts, about a hundred volunteers were trained. Of them, only a select few would participate in the campaign to liberate Dadra and Nagar Haveli. The rest were sent back to Goa to await further orders.[99]

Even though the training was rudimentary, the volunteers felt capable of handling themselves in a fight. Regular meetings between the Pune and Goa volunteers meant that everyone was on the same page and leaders of both groups were confident that they were quickly approaching combat readiness.

But then came news that placed a chokehold on their confidence. The Maharashtra Special Reserve Police, under instructions from the Government of United Maharashtra, had decided to throw a tight cordon around the occupied region, and Deputy Inspector-General J.D. Nagarwala had been put in charge of security. His brief was unambiguous—no one could enter or exit Dadra and Nagar Haveli without special permission and a good reason. These instructions aligned with Nehru's policy—no Indian was allowed to participate in any activity against the Portuguese. The situation, already quite grim, had just worsened.

---

99   Lawande, p. 168.

Making Friends

THE three groups had understood quite early on that liberating Dadra and Nagar Haveli could not be done without support at grassroots level. It was important to identify local people with influence who were sympathetic to the cause, and this task was now assigned to Appa Karmalkar by the Azad Gomantak Dal.

Karmalkar was an ex-employee of the Banque Nacionale de Ultramarino, which Lawande, Sinari and others had tried to rob without success a few years earlier. The Portuguese suspected Karmalkar of playing a role in the attempted robbery because of his close links with the Dal. Since they could not arrest him for lack of evidence, they transferred him to São Tomé and Principe, one of their African colonies. Convinced that accepting the transfer would mean being exiled from Goa for life, he fled to Bombay and took up a job at the United Commercial Bank. This also gave him the time and freedom to pursue his dream of liberating Goa from Portuguese occupation.[100]

It was Karmalkar who came up with the idea of combining forces with the volunteers from Pune.[101] Until now, his participation had been limited to the initial meeting at Phadke's residence in Bombay and the subsequent discussions during which a joint strategy for the attack had been finalised. This next stage was fraught with significant risk as there was a warrant for his arrest in Goa. Being caught would mean immediate detention and deportation. Yet, undeterred, he jumped into the fray and devoted himself to gathering local support.

The first person he reached out to was Jayantibhai Desai, a wealthy landowner from Dadra with nationalistic leanings who would play a significant role in the struggle, as well as in the post-liberation era. Desai's immediate contribution was putting Karmalkar in touch with Hemwatibai Natekar at the Tapovan Ashram in Lavachha.[102]

—

Lavachha was at the time a tiny rice-cultivating village situated on the narrow strip of land between Dadra and Nagar Haveli. About two kiometres from Dadra and barely four kilometres from the Portuguese headquarters of Silvassa, it was poorly connected by road with either place, and surrounded by dense jungle. The most prominent landmark in the area was

---

100 Lawande, p. 183.

101 Sinari, p. 110.

102 Letter from Appa Karmalkar to Jayantbhai Desai, 28 June 1954.

the Tapovan Ashram, and its best-known resident was the ashram's owner, Hemwatibai Natekar.[103]

A palatial, two-storey sloped-roof building surrounded by well-manicured lawns, the complex was bordered by forest on three sides and extensive rice plantations belonging to Hemwatibai on the other. A five-minute walk from the gate set into a tall boundary wall led to the main building, which was the residence of Hemwatibai. The annexe next to it housed the ashram, with its striking gold-painted dome visible even from a significant distance.

Although there was a temple dedicated to Lord Dattatreya in the main building, and bhajans were often sung, Tapovan was not primarily a religious institution. It was a haven for tribal women exploited by the Portuguese soldiers, officials and their local cohorts. Oppressed women from the occupied territories would cross the border to seek sanctuary here.

Additionally, it was a meeting place for prominent citizens from both sides of the border, which also made it the ideal place to contact them. A gathering of people from the Portuguese territories would ordinarily have attracted attention. At Tapovan, such gatherings were commonplace.

In fact, if there ever was a place designed to launch an attack on Dadra and Nagar Haveli, it was this ashram at Lavachha. Men could move quickly, and without being noticed, to and from the tiny strip of Indian land located between Portuguese territories. Since the ashram and the estate surrounding it employed many people, it was unlikely that the authorities would even notice the presence of a few more. All that was

---

103 Hemwatibai was tragically murdered in the mid-eighties over a property dispute. She left no direct heir but her family members donated the building to a trust, which still maintains it.

needed to take the team's plan forward was Hemwatibai Natekar's cooperation.

Natekar was a tall woman in her mid-forties, beautiful and dignified; a childless widow who treated her wards as her children. Her wealth was legendary—she was always dressed in nine-yard silk sarees, with diamond earrings and thick gold bangles. It was rumoured that, on special occasions, she served meals to her guests on plates of solid gold.[104] Her resources, though, were chiefly devoted to her cause.

The horror stories she had heard from the victims of Portuguese atrocities had already ignited her anger, which simmered just below the surface, waiting to find an outlet. When Desai introduced Karmalkar to her and she heard about their plans, she declared her support immediately.

To begin with, Karmalkar organised a meeting of prominent sympathisers to understand what kind of support could be expected from the residents of the occupied enclaves. The cover for the meeting would be an evening of bhajans sung by Sudhir and Lalita Phadke. Karmalkar asked Desai to coordinate with his local friends and ensure their attendance without mentioning the real reason for the meeting. Secrecy was still paramount.[105]

The Phadkes and Karmalkar left Bombay by train at 4.00 p.m. and got off at Vapi around 7.00 p.m.[106] It was raining heavily when the train drew into the station, and they were

---

104 Phadke, p. 220.
105 Letter from Appa Karmalkar to Jayantbhai Desai, 28 June 1954.
106 Ibid.

drenched as soon as they alighted. They had thought they were prepared for the weather, but the wind blew so fiercely that it was impossible to even open their umbrellas. Desai, who had arrived in a car to collect them, strongly advised them to stay the night at Vapi.

On the morning of 27 June, they left for Lavachha. They passed Portuguese-occupied Dadra on the way, but stayed within Indian territory. The checks at the Indian police posts were perfunctory, since Desai was well-known to the guards. Only when the car stopped near the jungle's edge did they understand why Desai had insisted on staying on in Vapi the previous night.

Tapovan, he explained, was located off the main road. Though it was possible to get there by car, the road connecting it to Vapi passed through Portuguese-occupied Dadra. While he could have got road permits for Lalita and Phadke, Karmalkar might have been arrested.[107]

Following his advice, they stepped off the road onto a narrow jungle trail and sent the car back. The canopy formed by the teak and rosewood trees cast shadows on the path and the thick undergrowth obstructed visibility. They walked for half an hour, relying on the tribal guide Desai had arranged for them. The pods that dropped from the khair and mahara trees crunched under their feet. Initially, the trail was somewhat even, but after a while, it sloped off, and they had to hold on to each other to avoid slipping. The journey, treacherous enough by day, would have been impossible to attempt on a rainy night. The trail ended at the edge of Natekar's rice plantation, after which they had to walk over the narrow embankments that kept the water in the flooded patches of

---

107 Bhikubhai Pandya, *Brief History of Liberation of Dadra and Nagar Haveli*, Souvenir Golden Jubilee Celebrations, 1998, p. 1.

rice from flowing out. It was a challenge, requiring them to wade through slush, and the group of four reached Tapovan weary and mud-splattered.

They were warmly welcomed by Natekar herself. After a bath and a hot meal, they sat down to discuss the task at hand. Desai and Natekar went through the names of possible local accomplices and, after some deliberation, drew up a list of potential supporters. A cordial invitation was extended to everyone on this list for a 'musical programme' being organised at Tapovan.

The event, although a cover, was a success. Phakde sang a few Marathi bhajans to begin with and then later, since a majority of the audience spoke Gujarati, he sang a few in that language as well. Lalita joined in towards the end, and though there was no one to play the tabla, their performance drew thunderous applause. When asked if he would sing again the following day, Phadke said it would depend on how they reacted to what he had to say next. Desai then explained in Gujarati why the Phadkes were there, and a hush descended on the gathering. Mercifully, when asked to retire to an inner hall for further discussion, not one of the guests walked away. They listened rapt as Phadke explained the plan to them in Hindi.[108]

'We need your help,' he said. 'Volunteers will come from outside for the attack. You will not have to participate, but we cannot do it without your support. I take full responsibility for your safety.'

Many pledged their support immediately, while some said they would think it over. Desai then asked Phakde to accompany him to Silvassa, where they could meet more

---

108 Phadke, p. 220.

potential supporters. Itching to see what Silvassa was like, Phadke and Lalita agreed.

They left Tapovan the next day at 10 a.m. They were stopped at the border by the Portuguese police, who gestured aggressively at the Phadkes and demanded to know who they were and why they were entering Nagar Haveli without documents. A brief explanation from Desai in Gujarati silenced them, and they waved the car through. Desai's story to them was that Phadke was due to sing at Lavachha in the evening but had developed a nasty cough. He said it was a medical emergency, and that they were going to Silvassa to see a doctor. But it was a narrow escape.

The meetings in Silvassa went well. Although some, like Desai's brother, refused to help for fear of the consequences, others were happy to.[109]

Phadke and Karmalkar made a few more trips to Lavachha and gradually, a plan began to take shape. Prominent local citizens like Bhikubhai Pandya, Guman Singh Solanki, Vanamali Bhavasar and Carlos DeCruz became associated with the struggle. They would not participate in the attack itself but would pass on information about the number of policemen at various stations, the weapons they carried, their routes, etc. Desai and Pandya set up communication lines, obtained information through the locals and collated it in Lavachha before forwarding everything to Karmalkar.[110]

This information was, however, often patchy and incomplete. They realised then that a detailed survey was necessary to understand the precise positions of the Portuguese and mark out viable approach routes to the police

---

109 Ibid.

110 Letters from Appa Karmalkar to Jayantbhai Desai, 26 June 1954, 31 July 1954.

posts. Since it was dangerous for volunteers from the Dal to enter Portuguese territories, this task was assigned to the Pune group.

When the group gathered to discuss the matter, everyone agreed that accurate information was vital to the plan's success. They had grown up on stories of Shivaji and how he had vanquished armies mightier than his own by using 'ganimi kava' or guerrilla tactics.[111] If they were to defeat the numerically superior, better-armed and well-entrenched Portuguese using similar tactics, knowledge of the terrain and of the strengths and weaknesses of the enemy was essential. Senior members of the group would have to visit the territories in disguise, it was decided, in order to gather intelligence. This would not only ensure the reliability of the data but also familiarise the group's leaders with the local topography, crucial for[112] rapid and strategic decision-making when leading the volunteers into battle. Wakankar, Kajrekar, Vaidya and Raman Gujar were entrusted with this responsibility.

111 Purandare, Visheshank, p. 13.
112 Ibid, p. 32.

Reconnaissance

T HE bangle seller slipped into Dadra without any difficulty. The border guards inspected his wares and waved him through, finding nothing suspicious. It was, after all, the month of Shravan, and it was customary for young women to buy bangles during this season. The cry of 'Bangdi laiylo, bangdi!' (bangles, get bangles!) echoed through the streets in all the villages and towns and you would often see men with their colourful wares, seated on the ground with women gathered around them.

Wakankar was dressed like any of the other bangle sellers. He had been making his way through the villages, pretending to do business while taking note of the roads, the police posts, telephone lines, power lines, and so on. He ventured out only during the hours when the womenfolk were too busy to look at the bangles on offer. However, on the third day, his luck ran out. As he reached a village near the town of Pipariya, an elderly woman sitting on the porch of her house noticed him and asked to see his goods. Reluctantly, he obliged. Liking what she saw, she called out to her daughters and daughter-in-law, asking them to choose some bangles for themselves. As he sat on the mud-floored courtyard of the hut surrounded by the women of the house, with the bangles spread out before him, Wakankar panicked. Not only was he unable to answer the questions they put to him, but when he had to hold the arm of the daughter-in-law of the house, his hand began to shake. As he slipped a bangle onto her wrist, it slipped, fell and broke into pieces. The other women started giggling, and the old lady realised something was wrong. 'Whoever you are, you're surely not a bangle seller,' she said and threatened to call the menfolk. His cover blown, Wakankar ran from the place with his bag full of bangles, exiting Nagar Haveli as fast as his legs could carry him. His career as a spy was over before it had begun.[113]

The incense-stick sellers were luckier because their preparation was more thorough. When Gujar and Kajrekar entered Nagar Haveli as sales representatives of a Pune-based company, they carried samples, bills and challan books bearing invoices for shopkeepers. A relative of Gujar owned a unit that had been manufacturing and supplying incense sticks to shops in Dadra and Nagar Haveli for several years, so their story was believable.

They patrolled the area for two days on the first trip, returning twice for further reconnaissance. Each time, the effort was to gauge the attitude of the local population towards their rulers. Finding enough evidence of dissatisfaction, they concluded that there would be little resistance if anyone did attempt to throw out the Portuguese.

---

113 Purandare, Visheshank, p. 32.

More importantly, they completed the task Wakankar had abandoned and noted the location of the remaining police posts, the numbers deployed and the available weapons. Kajrekar and Gujar made detailed sketches of entry and exit points to the various towns and villages and identified places to take cover near police stations. They marked choke points near highways from where access to Silvassa could be shut down. They also identified the phone lines which could be cut to disrupt communication to and from the capital city.[114]

What remained now was to gather information regarding the town of Silvassa itself, where the central garrison, as well as the offices of the administrator, Captain Fidaldo, and Lieutenant Falcao, the police chief, were located. Security was high in this area, so an unshakeable cover was required. It came from an unlikely source: Lalita Phadke.

Lalita had been born into a typical Chittapavan Brahmin family in 1925 and had inherited the extremely fair complexion of her clan. A successful singer in the Marathi film industry, she had gradually eased out of playback singing after marrying Phadke in 1949, though she continued to sing with her husband at concerts. She now came up with the idea of entering Silvassa in the guise of a college student and photographing police posts and other vital installations. Dressed in a skirt and blouse, her hair tied in two braids and mangalsutra tucked away, she could pass for a girl out on a picnic with a fancy new camera. Although she would be well out of her comfort zone, Lalita was determined to make the plan work. She knew it was the group's best chance to learn more about the town.[115]

---

114 Purandare, Visheshank, p. 32.
115 In conversation with Shreedhar Phadke.

And she did succeed—with one near miss. She went about town, snapping photos of the rivers, churches, temples and people. While photographing the town square, she also snapped a few pictures of the Silvassa police post. The guard on duty noticed this and rushed over, but seeing a harmless-looking college girl, he merely warned her off and attempted to confiscate the camera. Knowing the game would be up if she handed it over, she flew into a rage and tossed the camera on the road. In a shrill and tearful voice, she screamed at the guard, accusing him of misbehaving and taking advantage of a lone young woman. The guard recoiled, panicked by the unexpected verbal assault. Visibly embarrassed, he picked up the camera and, handing it back to her, advised her to leave before his seniors noticed her.[116]

Now, the team not only had maps and topographical details of the areas surrounding Silvassa, they also had photographs of the police post. They still needed information on how many policemen the city housed, how they were armed and the points of entry least likely to be guarded. So they decided to send out volunteers masquerading as beggars.[117] Shantaram Vaidya and two old friends of Kajrekar, Pilajirao Jadhavrao and Vishnupant Bhopale, volunteered to beg in the main square of Silvassa.

~

The two-storey building in the main square of Silvassa was known as the office of the chief of police but was effectively the district's headquarters as it also housed the administrator's office. It was a majestic building with a mud-tiled sloping

116 Joshi, p. 59.
117 Ibid.

roof in the front and a flat roof in the rear. There were two staircases that went up to the first floor, converging from opposite sides onto a landing leading to a wide verandah and the main offices as well as the record room and the treasury. The armoury, the police station and the jail were on the ground floor. From a post right opposite the building flew the Portuguese national flag.

At the back of the building was an open courtyard enclosed by a fifteen-foot-high wall with a sturdy wooden door embedded in it, which was kept locked most of the time. On the first floor, a verandah ran along the front and the back, approachable from the offices or a narrow staircase from the rear courtyard. The terrace on top of the structure could be reached via a small staircase leading up from the hall in the main building, or a rusty fire escape that ran along the outer wall of the building.

The main road from Dadra passed through Lavachha, past the Pipariya bridge over the Daman Ganga, and ended at Khanvel. Another road from Naroli joined this road to form the town square. A few small shops and the homes of Fidaldo, Falcao and other officials clustered around this square, and a path led away from it to the homes of prominent citizens and the church. The rest of the population of about 10,000 lived on either side of the main road.

It was in the town square, right opposite the police chief's office, that Vaidya and Jadhavrao sat down to beg, while Bhopale hung around as backup.

The Portuguese had strict rules about begging on the streets. Beggars were routinely rounded up and soundly thrashed. On the first day, these beggars too were chased away after a stern warning. When they reappeared on the second day, they were beaten with lathis. On the third day, Vaidya and Jadhavrao achieved their objective—they were arrested and hauled off to jail. They expected to be detained for a day, thrashed and let off, by which time they would have got the information they needed. However, things did not work out that way.

The Portuguese had realised that these were not ordinary beggars. They kept the two men handcuffed at all times and they were interrogated, beaten and threatened. Who were they? Why were they pretending to be beggars? What were their true intentions? Frustrated by their refusal to part with any information, the Portuguese officers beat them mercilessly.

Three days passed. When the police could not extract anything meaningful from them, Falcao ordered that they be transferred to Goa. Luckily, a policeman friendly to the cause informed Vaidya and Jadhavrao about this in time for them to think of a way out.

They knew that escape was vital and immediate, but it was impossible to attempt as long as their hands and feet were tied. The only time they were untied was in the morning, when they used the toilet. Even then, the handcuffs were not taken off; the two men were shackled together with a single pair of cuffs. Realising that this was the only chance they would ever get, on the fourth day of their detention, Vaidya and Jadhavrao scaled the toilet wall and escaped. Bhopale, who had been informed of the plan by the friendly policeman, was waiting for them behind the police station. The guard, meanwhile, waited outside the toilet in vain; it would be a few minutes before he discovered their escape.

Their options were limited—they could either run into the jungle chained together or enter the town and find someone who could get their handcuffs off. Either plan was risky. If they ran handcuffed, they would be able to get further away from the police post before the Portuguese discovered their escape, but any casual observer would know they were escaped prisoners. If they waited in town to get the handcuffs removed, they would be within Portuguese territory, and vulnerable. Without wasting any more time, they decided to go with the second option.

Breaking the handcuffs entailed finding an ironsmith, and Bhopale went looking for one. However, as he could not explain why he wanted his services, the man refused to accompany him. Bhopale had no patience for this. A seasoned wrestler, he placed the ironsmith in a chokehold and dragged him to the place where Jadhavrao and Vaidya were hiding. Two strokes with a hammer and chisel and the cuffs were off. They tied up and gagged the ironsmith, and fled to the jungle.

As they ran, they heard a cry go up—their escape had been discovered! All three raced towards the undergrowth as a Portuguese sergeant in khaki shorts, accompanied by three policemen with rifles, emerged from the police station and ran towards them, waving a revolver. He fired at the fleeing men and a bullet grazed Vaidya's back, but he ran on, paying no heed to the pain. By the time the policemen took up positions and cocked their rifles to fire at the runaways, they had disappeared into the undergrowth. Travelling by night and hiding by day, they reached Lavachha the next morning.[118]

The news they had escaped with was chilling. There were over 200 policemen in the Silvassa police station, armed with rifles, hand grenades and light machine guns.[119]

———

The group met in Pune towards the end of July to collate all the information they had gathered and decide on a possible course of action. Vaidya drew a map that indicated the

118 In conversation with Captain Sanjay Vaidya.
119 Purandare, Visheshank, p. 22.

positions of the various police posts on the road to Silvassa. After studying it, they agreed that they would first focus their attention on Dadra, which was separated from Nagar Haveli by a strip of Indian territory, and then enter Nagar Haveli from Naroli. After capturing Naroli, they would take Pipariya and march on to Silvassa with the weapons they managed

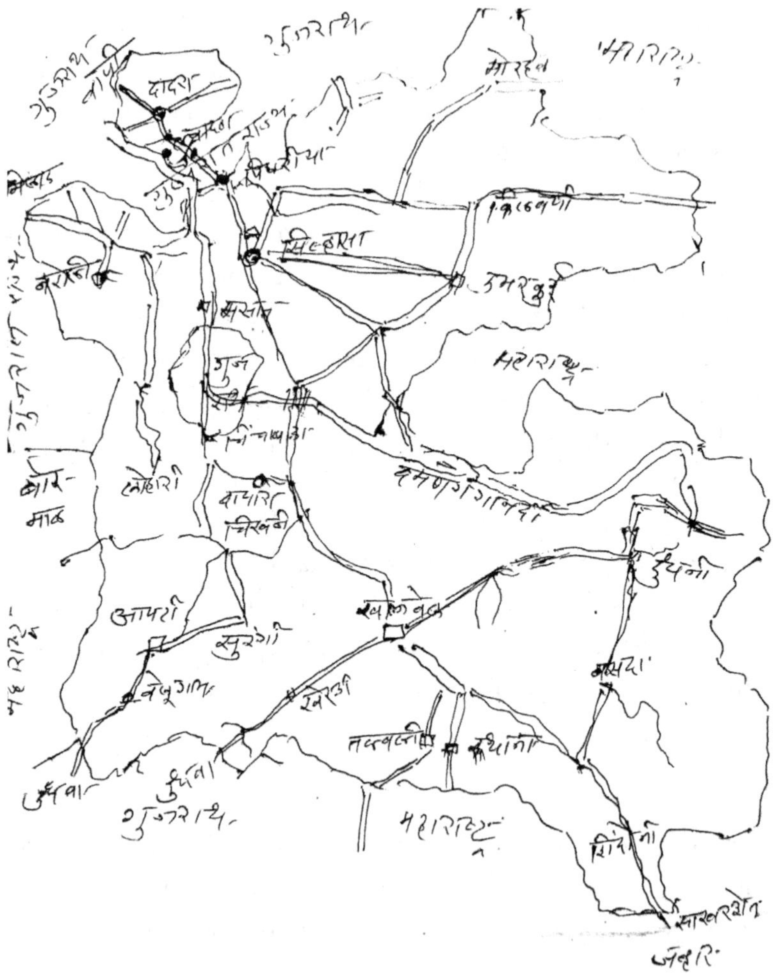

Rough map of the entire region of Dadra and Nagar Haveli drawn up by Shantaram Vaidya based on information collated following reconnaissance

to seize from each of the police posts. Since their numbers would not exceed thirty, even including the volunteers of the Azad Gomantak Dal, they decided to get reinforcements from Pune for the final assault. Wakankar spoke to Vinayakrao Apte, the regional head of the RSS, and he agreed to organise a team of boys who would ready to move when required.

The meeting identified two primary areas of concern. The first was the possibility of Captain Fidaldo getting reinforcements from Daman. For this, the Portuguese would require permission from the Indian government to pass through Indian territory as there was a thirty-five-kilometre stretch of land separating Daman from Nagar Haveli. The group believed that once it was evident that Indian citizens had participated in the rebellion, the Portuguese were sure to ask for a right of way, so they could send troops in. And if enough international pressure was applied, Nehru might well agree to the demand.

The second matter was of urgent concern too: an assessment of the strength of the garrison at Daman.

This time, Tryambak Bhat accompanied Wakankar. They found the easiest way to get into Daman without any documents—they simply told the border guard they wanted a drink.

In the 1950s, Maharashtra and Gujarat were joined together as a cohesive administrative unit called the Bombay State. Its chief minister, Morarji Desai, had enforced prohibition across the state in keeping with his puritan ideology, and soon, it became common for people to nip into Daman for a drink. On that day, the two well-dressed businessmen winked at the guard who had stopped them and told him they were looking forward to a bit of relaxation. Knowing what that meant and being used to such crossings, the guard waved them on with the warning that they would have to be back before sunset.

As they strolled towards the market, Wakankar noticed a border guard tailing them. So, he turned into the nearest bar and sat down and ordered drinks for two of them. The guard's suspicions were allayed and with a friendly nod, he turned away.

Later, Wakankar and Bhat walked around town, stopping sometimes to enquire about the price of fruit and conversing with random strangers on the street. They soon realised that the Portuguese were better prepared to defend Daman than Dadra and Nagar Haveli. There were many more policemen and soldiers, and they seemed better equipped. If reinforcements from here were to reach Silvassa, there was no chance of defeating the Portuguese or even escaping unscathed. They decided that cutting Daman's communication lines would have to be their top priority before attacking Silvassa. They simply could not afford an information leak that might alert the governor of Daman.

The two men made it back before the deadline given by the guard, but not before they went into a bar and had another glass of the local brew. The guard smelt it on them and let them pass without comment. This was probably the first and only time they entered a bar or touched a glass of liquor to their lips.[120]

The group withdrew to Pune to make plans for the final assault, leaving Kajrekar in Lavachha to keep an eye on things and update them.

---

120 Shashikant Mandke, *Dadra Nagar Havelichi Mukti*, Pushpa, Pune, 2008, p. 29.

Dadra

T HE ashram at Lavachha had a new gardener—Kajrekar, alias Nansingh bhaiya. He had stationed himself there to keep an eye on the border and was soon going in and out of Dadra so often, with the help of Jayantbhai Desai, that even the border guards no longer stopped him. He also befriended Aniceto Rosario, the sub-inspector in charge of the police post in Dadra, and often dropped by to play cards with him.

The plan was for Kajrekar to stop by for a game of cards on the day of the attack. Taking Rosario by surprise, he would snatch the submachine gun and capture the post. Desai assured Kajrekar he would get the support of the local nationalists when this happened.[121]

But before he could implement the plan, a series of events occurred in Goa and Bombay which would completely change the nature of the battle.

---

121 Kajrekar, p. 46.

In Goa, the United Goans (also known as the United Front of Goans) led by Francis Mascarenhas, former Indian counsel to Cuba, and his accomplice Vaman Desai, decided to attack and liberate Dadra. Though small, newly established—and quickly forgotten by history—the left-leaning group was closely aligned with the Communist Party under Godavaribai Parulekar. Its members were also close to Lohia and the socialists in the Indian National Congress. They used this connection to pressure Morarji Desai to grant them access to Dadra through Indian territory.

Since the liberation of the Portuguese-occupied territories was the responsibility of the citizens of those areas according to the Indian government, Morarji Desai was inclined to help them. He met Dr Harisinh Parmar and Amubhai Khira, both prominent citizens of Dadra, and requested them to support the United Goans. He also liaised with the railway ministry in Delhi to arrange for a special railway compartment for the Goans to travel to Vapi.

He then instructed the chief secretary of Maharashtra to contact the district collector of Surat and ask him to render all possible assistance to the Goans. The collector, in turn, got in touch with S.G. Gokhale, the district superintendent of police, and told him, in no uncertain terms, to 'Render all possible assistance, but under no circumstances should Indian police forces or civilians enter Dadra or Nagar Haveli.'[122]

Gokhale found these instructions difficult to comprehend. 'What if the Portuguese send reinforcements from Daman? Are we supposed to stop them? Is the use of force permitted?' he asked the collector. The collector, having no answer, passed the question back to Gokhale, asking him to take a call as

---

122 S.G. Gokhale, *Sangram*, Manohar Sadashiv Nirgude, Pune, 1995, p. 105.

he thought fit. Gokhale then wrote a detailed report, which he sent via a messenger to J.D. Nagarwala, deputy inspector-general in the Maharashtra police and a close confidant of Morarji Desai. Nagarwala grasped the seriousness of the issue and the consequences should the Portuguese decide to send reinforcements from Daman or Nagar Haveli. It would be a breach of territorial integrity unacceptable to India, but blocking the troops by force would cause international outrage. He spoke to Morarji Desai and, with his permission, despatched more units of the State Reserve Police to Vapi, and reached Lavachha himself to take charge of the operation.

Nagarwala discussed the matter with Colonel Jadhav, the officer in charge of the State Reserve Police, and his deputy, Major Shirole, and ordered the troops to dig deep trenches along the borders of Daman and Nagar Haveli. These would prevent Portuguese vehicles from crossing into Indian territory. He also ordered that a cordon be formed along India's border with Daman and Nagar Haveli to thwart any movement there.[123]

When Jayantibhai Desai heard of these plans, he summoned Kajrekar to Dadra. They convened a meeting of the local nationalist groups and appraised them of the situation. Jayantibhai also read out the message from Nagarwala requesting the villagers to cooperate fully with the United Goans. The mood was tense and angry. The group could not understand the motivation of the Indian government, which had until then discouraged any action against the Portuguese. Why was it so keen to ensure the success of the Goans? Kajrekar was doubly concerned as he saw months of hard work by his group and the Azad Gomantak Dal go to waste, and proposed that they pre-empt the attack by liberating

---

123 Ibid.

Dadra a day before the Goans arrived. The logic was that once they took over the police post and hoisted the Indian tricolour, the Goans would be forced to retreat. Kajrekar was confident that Nagarwala would then intercede on behalf of the RSS and Azad Gomantak Dal with Morarji Desai, and they would get the government's support for the attack on Nagar Haveli.[124]

The Dadra police post was a single-storey hutment-like structure a little off the main road that connected Vapi to Lavachha and Silvassa. Located on slightly higher ground, in a clearing surrounded by dense shrubbery, it comprised three rooms with huge windows and just one central entrance. The Portuguese flag flew in the area in front of the main entrance, and the grounds were large enough for only about forty or fifty people to gather.[125] The nearest house was that of Jayantibhai Desai, about 100 yards away.

At dusk on 20 July, Kajrekar, whom everyone there knew as Nansingh bhaiya, arrived at the Dadra police post for a game of rummy with Rosario. The card game was soon in full swing, and with a bottle of whiskey putting everyone at ease, the constables also joined the revelry. Excusing himself momentarily, Kajrekar stepped out to give final instructions to the volunteers from Dadra, who were gathered outside the post. He told them that he would move swiftly to stun Rosario, then take control of the Sten gun. While he held off the constables with it, the others should storm in and disarm them. They would then lower the Portuguese flag and host

---

124 Kajrekar, p. 45.

125 Whereas most landmarks associated with this era have been demolished and new buildings erected in their place, the Dadra police post still stands exactly as it was then. Even the house of Jayantibhai Desai still stands as before, though no one lives there now.

the tricolour, which Kajrekar carried wrapped around his body under his shirt.

But as Kajrekar turned to re-enter the police post, there was a commotion amidst the shrubs around the post. Shots whizzed past him, there were loud explosions, and armed men emerged from the shrubbery and rushed towards the post—the Goans had arrived a day early!

There was complete chaos; no one knew what to do. The volunteers who had assembled under the leadership of Jayantibhai Desai were caught in the crossfire and scattered in all directions. Kajrekar and Desai ran to the latter's house for shelter; their plan had collapsed.

Sadly, the assault by the Goans failed too. They had attacked without the slightest intelligence about the number of men at the post, the arms they carried, or even the entry and exit points. The consequence of such poor preparation was a disorganised and chaotic retreat into Indian territory.

With both plans of emancipating Dadra having been foiled, they were back to square one. Or worse off, since Rosario was now on the alert.[126]

Rosario spent all of the next day trying to communicate with the police station in Silvassa. But the Goans had cut the telephone lines the previous night. Eventually, he despatched a constable in civilian clothes with orders to cross the border and get the message across to either Silvassa or Daman, but the border police stopped him and sent him back. By evening, Rosario knew that if another attack were to occur, he would have to defend the post himself. So, he decided to seek the

126 Kajrekar, p. 45.

help of the villagers and sent a message to Jayantibhai to gather all the able-bodied men of the village at the police post.

Desai had been observing Rosario's activities from a distance. He knew the constables were being vigilant—they had boarded up the windows, mounted the Sten gun on a tripod, and placed it right in the middle of the main gate. Anyone launching a frontal attack on the police post would come directly into the line of fire.

Nevertheless, Kajrekar and Desai felt they might have a second chance. They directed their volunteers to join the villagers who were gathering in front of the police post. Getting the staff to lower their guard was no longer possible. But they knew they were not suspects in Rosario's eyes and hoped to use this to somehow turn the odds in their favour. The chance of success was low, but it was a risk worth taking.

At dusk, around 150 men gathered at the entrance of the police post. For the first time that day, Rosario stepped out from his position behind the Sten gun to address the villagers. Standing in the light of the lanterns they carried and the single naked bulb suspended over the main gate,[127] he assured them that they were safe, and explained what would be done in case of an attack. As he spoke, his gaze lingering on several familiar faces, he swelled with confidence and warned them fiercely against supporting 'terrorists'.

Kajrekar, Desai and their supporters were prepared to wait for the right opportunity, but unbeknownst to them, the Goans were back and observing the gathering from a distance. Seeing that Rosario had stepped away from the post, they closed in, crawling through the undergrowth to avoid

---

127 Joshi, p. 62.

being noticed. Four of them joined the crowd, their weapons concealed under the blankets draped around their shoulders.

Although he appeared confident, Rosario was under great stress, aware as he was that defending Dadra with just four policemen was impossible. His eyes darted all over the gathering as he spoke. At some point, he noticed that a fair number of newcomers in the crowd had blankets draped over their shoulders. Instinctively, he broke off mid-sentence, turned and rushed back into the post. Kajrekar, who had sidled up to him, followed close behind. The Goans realised their cover was blown and fired their weapons into the air, possibly to add to the chaos. As the villagers panicked and bolted for cover, the Goans chased Rosario down. Rosario managed to reach the gun, but did not immediately fire. His hesitation was fatal—one of the Goans stabbed him and he fell to the ground, bleeding profusely. One of the four guards on duty, Mohammad Khan from Dadra, dropped his rifle and surrendered. The other two, Clemente Francisco Pereira and Antonio Joaquim Francisco Fernandes, both from Daman, tried to escape with their weapons but were caught.

The United Goans were now in charge of Dadra.

Kajrekar and Jayantibhai backtracked swiftly into the bushes, but the Goans, assuming they were Portuguese supporters, sniffed them out within minutes. While the Goans let Jayantibhai go since he was a local, they bound Kajrekar in ropes and presented him to their leader, Francis Mascarenhas, who refused to accept his plea that he too was a freedom fighter. Dismayed, he cast around for help and noticed that the Goans were looking for an Indian flag to hoist. He turned to his captors and asked that they untie him briefly, so he could give them the flag he carried wrapped around his body. Threatening to shoot him down if he tried one false move, they retrieved the flag beneath his shirt and hoisted it. The villagers, who had been in a state of panic until now, took heart on seeing the tricolour fluttering in the breeze. They gathered in the square and saluted the flag. Jayantibhai then sent a messenger to Nagarwala, conveying the news of Kajrekar's arrest, and Nagarwala swiftly despatched two officers to confirm his identity with the Goans and escort him back to Indian territory.[128]

Meanwhile, the governor of the provinces of Daman, Dadra and Nagar Haveli, upon hearing of the attack, left for Daman to reclaim it. However, the trenches dug by the Special Reserve Police along the border stopped his cavalcade. When he attempted to march towards Dadra on foot, the border guards turned him away. The situation in Dadra, they said politely, was so uncertain that they could not guarantee his safety.

The Portuguese sent an official communiqué to the Indian government asking for right of passage for its armed personnel through Indian territory, which the Indians promptly rejected. The Indian stand was that some unarmed volunteers had tried to enter Dadra and the Portuguese police had fired at them. Incensed, the local population had risen against the police and taken over the administration. The action was not a hostile invasion by 'armed mercenaries' as the Portuguese asserted, but a people's uprising. There had been no external attack on Portuguese sovereignty, insisted the Indian authorities, and they would not support any action against the freedom fighters.

On 23 July, Mascarenhas held a press conference at the police post to announce that he would soon begin consultations with the 600-plus residents of Dadra and invite them to elect a gram panchayat. 'The panchayat,' he said, 'will run the

---

128 Kajrekar, p. 45.

administration under the supervision and control of a chief administrator appointed by the United Goans.' At the end of the meeting, the portraits of General Fransisco Lopes and Antonio Salazar, president and prime minister of Portugal, respectively, were taken down from the walls. A picture of Mahatma Gandhi replaced them to the accompaniment of loud cheers from all those who were present there.

A panchayat was soon elected, with Goan leader R.V. Rudra appointed as the administrator and Jayantbhai Desai as the sarpanch.

Dadra was finally free.

Backchannel Murmurs

EMBOLDENED by their success in Dadra, the United Goans now planned to seize the seventy villages of Nagar Haveli Pargana. Though their leader, Godavaribai Parulekar, did not have the support of the government, she had the backing of the Warli and Kokna tribals. Led and inspired by her, a thousand tribals marched into Nagar Haveli using little-known jungle trails. They hoisted the tricolour in the villages of Narkhed and Ranchirai on 3 August 1954. Then they marched to Randha and Pilwani, to the northeast of Silvassa, and declared those hamlets free. Six of the seventy-two villages in the province, including the two in Dadra, were now independent.[129]

On 9 August, the Goan People's Party, which was directly aligned with the Communist Party, held a press conference in Bombay and claimed that their volunteers had liberated some more villages in the past two days. George Vaz and Narayan

---

129 *Hindustan Times*, 5 August 1954.

Palekar asserted that sixty-three of the seventy villages of Nagar Haveli, besides the two in Dadra, were now under their control.[130]

Government circles in Bombay were certain this was mere bluster; it could not be that virtually all of Nagar Haveli was free. And they were right. None of the police posts, such as Naroli, Pipariya, Khanvel and Silvassa, were under the control of the Goan People's Party. They had declared all the non-policed hamlets free of Portuguese rule, which meant little. Yet, alarm bells rang in the corridors of power in Bombay, and Morarji Desai called a meeting with his trusted advisors.

Morarji Desai, then fifty-eight and one of the most senior leaders of the Indian National Congress, oversaw the Gujarati- and Marathi-speaking areas surrounding Dadra and Nagar Haveli. He would later become the finance minister under Nehru, the deputy prime minister on two occasions and the prime minister for two and a half years after the Emergency. He was a confirmed Gandhian, committed to khadi, strict about prohibition, and known for his views on development through the use of indigenous skills and production methods rather than the industry-led model Nehru was keen on. This resulted in considerable stress between the two and also to him being considered a harsh fanatic, whereas he was only a very solemn man.[131] He supported the Nehruvian policy of the people of the occupied territories being responsible for their own liberation but disliked the communists as he found their totalitarianism unacceptable.[132]

---

130 *Hindustan Times*, 9 August 1954.

131 Arvinder Singh, *Morarji Desai: A Profile in Courage*, Niyogi Books, New Delhi, 2019, p. 8

132 Singh, pp. 49–50.

Morarji Desai was in a particularly awkward situation in the days following Dadra's independence. He had to face the wrath of Nehru, who was upset about the violence in Dadra and the death of a police officer. At the same time, he feared that if the Communist Party managed to liberate the region, they might use it to launch an armed insurgency against the Indian state, as they had in Telangana following Hyderabad's merger with the Indian Union in 1948.

Added to this was the behaviour of the United Goans, who now controlled Dadra. There were allegations of looting, insolence towards women and a disregard for any instructions issued by the Indian administration. The local police and the district administration at Vapi and Surat were extremely upset with them, especially since the episode with the governor of Daman, when he had tried to enter Dadra. Vaz, Mascarenhas and their team had made plans to 'arrest' him when he landed at Vapi, ignoring the district police chief Gokhale's warning that this could create an international incident. Had the governor not been persuaded to return, the police knew they would have had to use force to restrain the Goans.[133]

Against this backdrop, and just a day before Morarji convened a meeting with his advisors in Mumbai, Shamrao Lad of the Azad Gomantak Dal, Phadke and Wakankar of the RSS and local citizens like Pandya and Solanki had a meeting with Nagarwala. They demanded permission to enter Nagar Haveli and wanted to know why his forces were preventing them from approaching the border when the government had directly supported the United Goans.[134]

Nagarwala agreed to speak with Morarji Desai. At the meeting in Bombay, also attended by the chief secretary J.

---

133 Gokhale, p. 106.
134 Mandke, p. 32.

Seth, he briefed the chief minister on Godavaribai Parulekar's plans to attack Silvassa. He expressed his inability to stop the tribals because of their sheer numbers and because they knew the jungle paths like the back of their hands. The only way to keep the situation under control, he said, was to disregard Nehru's directives. After some consideration, Morarji decided to heed this advice and permit the Azad Gomantak Dal volunteers to act.

He later justified the decision by saying, 'Within a year of Indian independence, the Communist Party has created rebellion-like situations in various parts of the country. I could see such a possibility arising in Dadra and Nagar Haveli. At that time, a group of satyagrahis approached me and asked permission to enter Nagar Haveli, which I granted, given the communist threat.'[135]

Nagarwala headed back to Lavachha, where he summoned Lad and Wakankar and gave them the go-ahead. He assured them of government cooperation on Indian soil, and promised them that reinforcements would not be allowed to reach Silvassa from Daman. He would increase patrolling on the border, he said, and mislead the Portuguese by letting them believe that the Special Reserve Police were planning to enter Nagar Haveli covertly. However, two things were non-negotiable, he told them. Firstly, the Indian forces would not enter Nagar Haveli at any cost, even if there was any danger to the volunteers' lives. Secondly, RSS volunteers would be allowed to join the fight only in their personal capacity; they would not be permitted to call themselves members of the 'Rashtriya Swayamsevak Sangh' or 'RSS'. This was in keeping with the general antipathy towards the RSS, especially among Congressmen. After the assassination of Mahatma Gandhi,

---

135 Joshi, p. 62.

the organisation had been formally banned by Union Home Minister Vallabhbhai Patel on 4 February 1948. The ban was lifted on 11 July 1949, after RSS chief Madhav Sadashiv Golwalkar gave an undertaking committing the organisation to a path of peace. However, the RSS continued to be perceived by many as the 'killers' of Gandhi.

Considering the cause to be much bigger than the taking of credit, Wakankar readily agreed to fight under the banner of the Azad Gomantak Dal.[136]

The die was cast.

---

136 Purandare, Visheshank, p. 22.

Naroli

THE speed with which the Desai government took the decision and communicated it to Wakankar and Lad was understandable. Pressure was mounting from all sides.

The United Goans under Mascarenhas and Vaman Desai had been sent back to Goa by the police due to their misconduct and indiscipline. They were smarting at this insult, and the ignominy of India withdrawing its support and summarily dismissing them. They now decided to join Godavari Parulekar and enter Nagar Haveli with her.

Godavari Parulekar was camped in the Thane district of Maharashtra, preparing the Warlis for the next attack. She had also visited Vapi to survey the area and explore the possibility of entering Nagar Haveli from that direction, but the Surat district police had detained her, and Gokhale had personally escorted her away from the border in his vehicle. However, soon after that, intelligence reports indicated that she had shifted base to Udhawa, north of Silvassa, and planned to make her move as soon as the monsoon abated.[137]

The Desai government feared that if the group succeeded, it would become impossible to dislodge the Communist Party from the area. The only viable option then was pre-empting the attack and swiftly liberating Nagar Haveli before Parulekar could act.

The liberation of Dadra had also sent alarm bells ringing in Portugal; there was news that Salazar had sought help from the USA and was seeking intervention by NATO. If Prime Minister Nehru got wind of Desai's plans, he might well order a halt to operations.

Immediate action was imperative for both these reasons, and both Wakankar and Lad responded promptly. On 23 July 1954, Wakankar sent a telegram to Pune directing the first batch of volunteers to head to Vapi with all available weapons. Over the next few days, from 25 July to 27 July, small batches of volunteers began to gather at Karambele near the border, where they set up camp in the Chinteshwar Mahadev temple,[138] while another batch assembled in the jungles near Lavachha.

Wakankar and Sinari discussed many alternate routes to Silvassa and came to the conclusion that the one they had previously decided on at a meeting in Pune was the best. They would enter via Bhilad, attack Naroli, the first major Portuguese police station, and then take the Pipariya police post. Controlling the Pipariya bridge would give access to the main highway leading to Silvassa, where the final battle would be fought.

Preparations began for the attack on the first target: Naroli.

---

137 Gokhale, p. 107.
138 Joshi, p. 63.

The next two days were spent arranging for supplies, testing each weapon and discussing strategy. On 28 July, word reached the volunteers via their Naroli informant Guman Singh Solanki that the Daman Ganga was overflowing and had flooded the road to Silvassa, cutting off access to Naroli. Solanki's assessment was that though nine constables armed with rifles and about 150 rounds of ammunition were posted at the police station, they were not likely to get any support from Silvassa because of the floods.[139] Based on this information, Wakankar and Sinari decided to attack Naroli immediately.

A total of twenty-nine volunteers equipped with rifles, pistols, hand grenades and knives left Karambele at 2 a.m. on 29 July. Vishnu Bhopale was, as usual, carrying his axe, which would turn out to be a game changer on at least two occasions in the following days.

It was raining heavily when they left. Visibility was low and the road was slippery. They had walked a kilometre in the rain when Wakankar suddenly saw a light flickering in the distance and stopped in his tracks. It was a Special Reserve Police post, and he had no idea whether the permission given to them by Nagarwala to enter Portuguese territory had been communicated to every checkpoint. Even if it had, the instinct of any sentry upon suddenly seeing a group of armed men emerge from the darkness would be to attack. To avoid that, the men opted to make their way through the jungle.[140]

If marching on the road in complete darkness and pouring rain had been bad enough, taking the jungle path proved to be worse. The trail was even slushier, and the volunteers had to wade through muck. Regardless of whether they

---

139 Lawande, p. 200.
140 *Loksatta*, 2 August 1979.

were wearing shoes or slippers, stones and thorns made their presence forcibly known.[141] But, guided by Ambalal Bhavasar, an associate of Jayantibhai Desai and a resident of Bhilad, they trudged determinedly through the sludge, often slipping and falling, but carrying on.

It was 4.30 a.m. when they crossed into Portuguese territory and encountered more hurdles. First, they came face to face with the Daroda River, a subsidiary of the Daman Ganga that was in full spate due to the heavy rains. Though the river was hardly thirty feet wide, the current was so strong that getting washed away was a distinct possibility. Anticipating this, the team had carried with them a thick coil of rope, and Pilaji Jadhav now volunteered to swim across with it. Holding one end of the rope, he swam to the opposite bank, where he tied it around the trunk of a tree. The others crossed the river by clinging to the rope. The crossing took forty minutes, and it was 5.30 a.m. when they reached Naroli.[142]

Their first stop was the house of Guman Singh Solanki. A short whistle brought him to the window. He gestured to them that all was clear and slithered down a drain pipe from his first-floor window to join them. He told them they had got lucky, as only six of the nine constables were on duty at the station that day.[143] The group spread out and stealthily approached their target, hardly 300 feet from Solanki's house.

The police station at Naroli was a single-storey building which doubled as the office of civil administration, also known as a patelado.[144] It was built in the typical Portuguese

141 Lawande, p. 201.

142 *Loksatta*, 2 August 1954.

143 In conversation with Yogendra Solanki in Silvassa.

144 Sinari, p. 79.

style, with a massive main door and three large windows on the sides and the rear. Right behind the police post, running parallel to the road, was the telephone line connecting Naroli to Silvassa.

At a signal from Bhopale, three volunteers gathered in a huddle. Two others climbed on their shoulders, and Bhopale, scampering up on top of them, used his axe to cut the wires. The post was now cut off from Silvassa.[145]

Kajrekar and Wakankar took up positions at the rear of the building. Bhatt, Lad and Jadhav were at the front while the others, led by Vaidya, lined up along the sides. Their instructions were clear—if anyone so much as peeped out of the building, he was to be shot dead.[146]

Kajrekar and Wakankar fired into the air simultaneously, and at the signal, the others began to fire at the building. As bullets ricocheted off the doors and windows, loud cries of 'Bharat mata ki jai!' and 'Azad Gomantak Dal zindabad!' ruptured the silence. The policemen fired back from inside, but sporadically, as they did not know who to aim at in the darkness. Then, in an audacious move, Sinari, with a pistol in each hand, rushed at the main door as Bhopale went to the side window and kicked it with immense force. The old window collapsed inwards with a thud.

Sinari fired at the main gate and shouted at the occupants to surrender or lose their lives. Stunned by the suddenness of the attack, four of the policemen threw down their rifles and came out with their hands raised. When the fifth raised his rifle to fire at Sinari, Bhopale hit him over the head with the rear end of his axe, and he crumpled to the floor. Wakankar, Kajrekar and the others rushed in and disarmed the sixth. The

---

145 *Loksatta*, 2 August 1979.
146 Joshi, p. 63.

remaining three policemen, who had been out in the village when the attack started, were also captured and brought back to the station.

Wakankar lined up all nine constables against a wall, while the team searched the premises. They seized nine rifles, six pistols and all the ammunition they could find. Mashadu Xavier, the only senior officer present, signed a note that said, 'The proposal of the Azad Gomantak Dal to run the administration of the areas … is acceptable to us. Therefore, I, along with my subordinates, do with this document surrender and hand over the possession of Naroli to the Azad Gomantak Dal.'[147]

By then, it was dawn, and the villagers started gathering outside the station, keen to know what had happened. In their presence, Lad hoisted the tricolour on the flag pole at the station and declared Naroli free. Lawande arrived within two hours and appointed Guman Singh Solanki as the sarpanch.

The volunteers then divided themselves into three groups. One stayed in the police station to defend Naroli; the second left with a local guide to secure the surrounding villages. The third, under Shantaram Vaidya, was despatched to the bridge over the Daman Ganga to prevent reinforcements from reaching Naroli.[148]

They now had to decide what to do with the police officers. Lad wanted to hold them under arrest at the police post itself, but the others demurred, since that would mean allocating scarce human resources to guarding them. So, they decided to hand the prisoners over to Nagarwala. Surprisingly, the suggestion came from the senior Portuguese officer, who said they would feel safe in the custody of the Indian police. It

147 Lawande, p. 202.
148 Lawande, p. 203.

is unclear whether this was because they did not trust the Dal volunteers or because they did not want to get caught in the crossfire of a counter-attack, but the team accepted the suggestion with alacrity and the prisoners were transferred to the Special Reserve Police. Nagarwala was initially reluctant because he had no official reason to detain them, but eventually he took them into custody for 'crossing into India without proper documents'.[149]

It soon became clear to Naroli's liberators that Silvassa could not be attacked with the less than fifty volunteers they had with them. They would have to fight 200 soldiers equipped with rifles, revolvers, Sten guns and machine guns. And without the element of surprise, the Portuguese would be difficult to take on.[150]

Just as the core group was pondering over what to do, the Dal volunteers who had escorted the prisoners into India returned with a message from Nagarwala. He wanted the leaders of the Dal to meet him on priority because he had information that the Parulekar group was planning to attack Silvassa on 1 August—and they had now been joined by the United Goans and Captain Dabholkar.

Captain Dabholkar, codenamed Captain Gole, was the chief instructor of the Dal. He had been the chief instructor at all the six training camps organised by the Dal for teaching its volunteers techniques of armed conflict and guerrilla warfare. Gole had also arranged for the purchase and serviceability of most of the arms that the Dal possessed,

---

149 Joshi, p. 65.
150 Ibid.

and taught the volunteers how to use and maintain them. He had also set up the Azad Goa radio after arranging for all the material components that were required through an Indian Navy officer. He had then persuaded a navy technician to assemble the parts and start the broadcast. Until now, he had been at the centre of all the activities of the Dal, so his moving to the Parulekar camp at this juncture was a big blow, and shocking to most of the Dal volunteers, who regarded him as a mentor.

Lawande, however, was not surprised—he had seen it coming. Gole had always been ideologically aligned with the left. The Dal had no objection to this because it was an umbrella body with adherents to different ideologies united by the common goal of liberating Goa and allied territories from Portuguese occupation. Lawande himself was a socialist, but he considered himself a nationalist first, and he saw nothing wrong with taking help from anybody, as long as it furthered the cause of the Dal. Therefore, when Lad and Karmalkar had originally proposed aligning with the RSS group in Pune, he had agreed. Gole, however, had been deeply disturbed by this as he believed that it was better for the Dal to align with the communists under Parulekar. When he saw that the RSS volunteers had taken on a prominent role in the campaign, he went to meet Lawande in Karambele. They spoke twice, first on 26 July 1954 and again on 28 July, just after the assault on Dadra by the United Goans. Both times, Gole tried to persuade Lawande not to have any truck with the RSS group.

Lawande's response was clear: 'The Azad Gomantak Dal welcomes in its fold every Indian who offers to help liberate Indian territories from Portuguese occupation. To us, all volunteers are volunteers of the Dal, and we do not like their flaunting any loyalty but to the Dal and its cause. You, yourself entered the Dal because you are an Indian first and not a member of any political party.'[151]

Lawande wanted Gole to continue working with the Dal as before and offered to appoint him as a section commander. But Gole refused and joined Godavari Parulekar, with whom he was already in touch. By this time, the Goan People's Party, an affiliate of the Communist Party of India, and the United Goans had also joined Parulekar.

Godavari Parulekar and her supporters now had a commander trained in jungle warfare, who was cognizant of the strengths and weaknesses of the Azad Gomantak Dal. With renewed confidence, and with 1 August as the target date, the group entered Nagar Haveli and set up camp at Rakholi, south of Silvassa.

The Dal urgently needed to get its act together or settle for being a mere footnote in the story of the liberation of Dadra and Nagar Haveli.[152]

⁓

Unknown to the Portuguese, two sympathisers of the Dal had infiltrated their police force. Rajendra Desai and Kashinath Desai, relatives of one of the Dal's founders, Dattaram Desai, had put in their applications when the Portuguese administration in Goa announced the recruitment of constables for Nagar Haveli. The Portuguese initially posted them in different police stations, but Falcao had summoned them to Silvassa along with all the other recruits after the fall of Naroli.

---

151 Translated from Marathi, Lawande, p. 209.
152 Lawande, p. 210.

Lawande sent two volunteers dressed as Warlis to contact the undercover cops in Silvassa. Cycling approximately sixteen kilometres to Silvassa and back, they returned the same day with the latest updates.

The atmosphere at Silvassa, they said, was one of fear; the Portuguese suspected that the Dal volunteers on the offensive were secretly officers of the Special Reserve Police. With all communications cut off, Captain Fidaldo, Lieutenant Falcao and his deputy Pegado had realised that reinforcements were not likely to come. Since they did not know the number of Dal volunteers on the move, they decided to not spread themselves thin; a solid defensive position was more desirable.

The two constables had also passed on the news that, with the focus on setting up a strong defence perimeter, Fidaldo had left only a token few officers at all the eight police stations under his control (the ninth being Naroli, now with the Dal) and recalled all the other policemen to Silvassa. Not content with that, he had redeployed all the forest and customs guards in Silvassa and armed them. The town square of Silvassa was deserted, and all the shops shut. In the police chief's office, the staircase that led to the first floor was no longer visible since a sixteen-foot-high wall of sandbags had been erected in front of it. The muzzles of Sten guns and rifles peeked out from slits between the sandbags. The policemen manned these guns in shifts, and the lights in the office blazed day and night.

Clearly, the chances of entering Silvassa police station by stealth were nil. The Dal needed more volunteers, and fast.[153]

---

153 Lawande, p. 211.

Wakankar, Phadke, Lawande, Karmalkar and Sinari sat down to discuss what was to be done next. They were in complete agreement that attacking the police headquarters at Silvassa, with its sandbagged defences and the number of armed, trained soldiers and police officers, was not a task the seventy-five volunteers could take on. However, they couldn't agree on what was to be done about the situation. While Lawande felt that regardless of the chances of success or the likely damage, an attack ought to be launched immediately with available resources, Wakankar and Karmalkar favoured inducting more volunteers to increase their chance of success. Lawande was sceptical about getting a hundred more volunteers on board within two days. He also wondered how helpful these untrained volunteers would be. 'Wouldn't they be like scarecrows?' was his question.[154]

Ultimately, Wakankar and Karmalkar prevailed, and they hurried to Pune on 29 July, burdened by the onerous responsibility of recruiting a hundred volunteers to enter a battle they would have neither heard of nor trained to participate in. And they had to do this in a single day.

They turned to the only source they knew that could arrange for the necessary volunteers at such short notice—the RSS. As a full-time volunteer for many years, Wakankar had close ties with the regional heads of the RSS, Babarao Bhide and Vinayakrao Apte. Karmalkar and he spoke with them about the current status of operations in Dadra and Nagar Haveli and the requirement for more men. Both RSS men got into action immediately and sent word to all the youth organisations they had connections with. Wakankar was already very popular amongst the youth due to his prowess at

---

154 Lawande, p. 213.

kabaddi and wrestling, and was able to summon many others from his network.

Bhide, Karmalkar and Wakankar went all over Pune to college hostels, RSS shakhas and gymnasiums, urging their friends to join them in a work of national importance that could, however, result in injury or even death. Despite not knowing the details, which were deliberately concealed from them, many volunteered, and recruitment went on well into the night of 30 July. Messengers were also sent to Nana Kajrekar's friends in Satara and Talegaon.

On the morning of 1 August, young men from various organisations assembled in front of the temple opposite the Shanivar Wada and were briefed about the nature of the mission. Fifty-four young men agreed to volunteer and took an oath to sacrifice their lives for the cause. They told their families they were leaving to attend a function organised by the RSS, and boarded the train to Vapi from Pune at 3.10 p.m. on the same day. Another group left from Talegaon, and friends of Kajrekar came from Satara. Most landed at night and were transported to Lavachha in vehicles arranged by the Special Reserve Police.

At Lavachha, some volunteers of the Azad Gomantak Dal from Goa also joined them. They gathered in the jungles near the estate of Hemwatibai Natekar. It had been raining without pause, and they were thoroughly drenched, with no change of clothes or a place to shelter from the rain. Natekar ensured they got tea and something to eat, so they were bedraggled but in high spirits. Still, it was a motley group, with hardly anyone having ever used a firearm. What they carried with them as weapons were sticks, the occasional knife and a sword or two.

At the last Indian checkpoint, a Special Reserve Police official warned them they were heading towards disaster. 'One trained soldier will be able to handle twenty of you,' he told them. 'I hope we don't have to enter Nagar Haveli in civil dress to bring back your corpses.' Undeterred, the group waited at the border, awaiting the signal to enter Portuguese territory and march towards Silvassa.[155]

Phadke and a few others were camping at the Chintan Mahadev temple in Karambele, from where the first group had left for Naroli. Based on the information they had, Phadke decided to head towards Silvassa immediately. But first, he met Nagarwala and obtained a note on his official letterhead that said, 'Allow Mr Phadke and his men to move freely inside.' The letter was additional insurance should any Indian officials who were unaware of the latest developments stop them inside Indian territory. Nagarwala also deputed a van equipped with a wireless set to accompany the team to the Portuguese border so they could contact him in case of any trouble.[156]

The group proceeded from Bhilad via the Bhilad–Naroli road and marched along for a few kilometres. Around 2.30 a.m., as they approached the border, it occurred to them that the danger of being accidentally shot by the Special Reserve Police was very real. How could the border guards know whether these men trudging along the highway with weapons in hand were to be stopped or let through? If they stopped the group, the letter could be shown, but what if they shot first and asked questions later? There was also the possibility that not every single police post had received instructions. After some discussion, they decided that taking the jungle

---

155 Joshi, pp. 59–60.
156 *Loksatta*, 2 August 1979.

path was a safer, if more challenging option. Phadke sent a final message to Nagarwala, returned the van, and then the group plunged into the jungle, heading for Naroli.[157]

Their first real obstacle was the Daroda, flowing even more fiercely than before. This time, Mohan Ranade, who had recently arrived from Goa, offered to swim across first. Just as he was tying one end of a thick rope to his waist, someone spotted a boat on the other side.[158]

They began to frantically call out to the boatman, who noticed them after much shouting and gesticulation and brought the flat-bottomed boat, locally known as a tar, across. It was a small boat and could only accommodate three or four people at a time. The boatman made many trips across, ferrying them in small batches. An hour later, they had all crossed over, and by 6.30 a.m. they were in Naroli. There, they joined Kajrekar's group, which was stationed at the Naroli police station. Kajrekar agreed with their decision to attack immediately and, together, they began the march to Silvassa.

There were now three groups of volunteers inside Portuguese territory. The first, led by Sinari, Kajrekar and Phadke, had entered via Bhilad and were marching to Silvassa along the Daman Ganga. The second was the group of new volunteers from Pune led by Wakankar, Lad and Lawande, who were moving along the Lavachha–Silvassa road. The third was the small group led by Shantaram Vaidya, whose job was to guard the Naroli–Pipariya road and ensure no reinforcements reached Naroli. It was this group that would go on to capture the Pipariya police station.[159]

---

157 Ibid.

158 Mohan Ranade, *Satiche Vaan*, Param Mitra Publications, Thane, 1969, p. 36.

159 Handwritten notes by Shantaram Vaidya, sourced from his son Captain Sanjay Vaidya.

Pipariya

Located on the main road connecting Lavachha to Silvassa, the Pipariya police station was strategically located as it guarded the Pipariya bridge,[160] a narrow stone bridge across the Phalandi, a minor tributary of the Daman Ganga. Located less than a kilometre from the Indian border and almost twice the distance from the town of Pipariya, it controlled access to Silvassa; the Pipariya gate was also called the gateway to Silvassa. It was a squat single-storey structure built at the edge of the bridge, with its back to Silvassa, facing the Indian border. Strangely, despite its importance, it was poorly maintained. A roof with tiles coming off, a worn-out wooden door in the front and two huge windows on the side (which looked almost ready to fall off) belied its significance as a post manned by as many as twenty men, led by two officers.

---

160 The Pipariya bridge is currently in a dilapidated condition and a new four-lane bridge had been built next to it. At the time of the field visits for the book, we were told it was due to be demolished.

Vaidya and Sinari realised that if their newest recruits marched down this road for the final attack, the Portuguese could fire directly at them from the police post. So, taking control of the post was necessary. Also, if the Portuguese sent reinforcements from Silvassa to stop the volunteers, control of the bridge could convert it into a choke point for them. By now, they had information that the first group of volunteers was in place, so they decided to act immediately.

Wakankar had put Vaidya in charge of this group before leaving for Pune. In consultation with Sinari, Vaidya divided the volunteers into four clusters. Vaidya and Vasant Badve approached the police post from the roadside, while Bhopale and Sinari crawled towards it from the riverside. Nana Soman and the others took up positions facing the bridge.

At a signal from Vaidya, Badve entered the police station through a half-open window. The window had a wooden rack resting against it from the inside and his attempt to push through caused it to crash to the floor. He stumbled, falling backwards onto the ground outside. The sound alerted the policemen inside, and when Badve made it through the window on his second attempt, he found five rifles pointed at him. A constable placed his bayonet against Badve's chest, and told him to turn around and drop his pistol. Soman, Sinari and the others, who had already entered through the side window and the front door froze in place, unwilling to endanger Badve's life. They too were ordered to drop their weapons.

Just when everything seemed lost, Vaidya leapt in through the window and, landing on the now fallen rack, thrust the bayonet of his rifle into the side of the policeman holding Badve hostage. As he collapsed in a pool of blood, the others overpowered the remaining constables.

After that, the officers quietly surrendered. They readily signed a surrender document and handed control to the Dal volunteers. Pipariya had fallen.[161]

The group seized five rifles with bayonets and 150 rounds of ammunition for each person who was part of the raid. Only later did they realise how lucky they had been—of the twenty policemen posted there, Falcao had withdrawn fifteen to Silvassa just a day before to shore up his defences. Had the station been fully staffed, the outcome would have been far bloodier.[162]

The capture of the police post was a milestone, but a shaky one, since reinforcements from Silvassa could quite easily reverse the situation. To prevent this, it was essential to hold the bridge until the entire Indian contingent assembled for the final assault. Accordingly, the twelve divided into two groups and hid in the dense grass in the pouring rain, near the Phalandi. They took positions on both sides of the narrow stone bridge, their rifles aimed at the entrance to the bridge from the Portuguese side. Hidden by the tall grass, they had the bridge covered. Vaidya instructed them to fire at anyone trying to cross over from the enemy side.[163]

Besides the roaring of the river and the chirping of the crickets, nothing was heard for hours. As they lay on the cold, wet ground, their adrenaline rush petering out, they realised they had not eaten for twenty-four hours. In Naroli, they had been provided food from Natekar's ashram in Lavachha, but here, they were utterly isolated. No one even knew they had

---

161 Sudha Karanjgaokar, *Mukti Sangram*, Bharatiya Itihaas Sankalan Samiti, Ahmedabad, pp. 98–99.

162 Joshi, p. 69.

163 Handwritten notes by Shantaram Vaidya, sourced from his son Captain Sanjay Vaidya.

taken Pipariya. And as there were only twelve of them to defend the bridge, there was no question of going across the border for food.

Madhu Punde, the youngest in the group, produced a few millet chapattis and onions he had brought with him. They ate half a chapatti each and settled back down on the watch. Just then, a cheer went up and slogans of 'Bharat mata ki jai!' were heard. The volunteers led by Phadke and Kajrekar had reached Pipariya![164]

When this group had left Naroli, they had been determined to march directly to Silvassa. If the reinforcements from Pune did not arrive on time, they were resolved, like the Lawande-led group, to team up with whoever was available and attack regardless of the consequences. With this in mind, they had marched towards Silvassa and reached the Daman Ganga, across which lay the capital.

Looking at Silvassa from a distance, they found it unusually quiet. There was no movement, no visible activity at all. Phadke and Kajrekar were immediately suspicious. Only two options presented themselves: the Portuguese lay in ambush, or the communists had already taken over. Given the reports that Parulekar planned to enter Silvassa on 1 August, the latter seemed most likely. From where they stood, a tin shed was visible across the river. Kajrekar lifted his rifle and let loose a barrage of bullets at it. He expected a return of fire if the Portuguese were in command or an appeal to stop firing by the communists. However, his firing spree was met with complete silence.

---

164 *Loksatta*, 2 August 1979.

They decided to investigate further, but the Daman Ganga was overflowing, and there was no bridge to cross over. Nor was swimming an option. Kajrekar turned to the two men from Naroli who had joined them after its liberation, hoping they might know what to do. And they did.

Leading the others further upstream, these men indicated a point where several rocks lay submerged and barely visible in the riverbed. Rubble had been piled up over them in places to make a temporary bridge. This was the path the locals usually took to cross over. The rain had subsided by then, and some of the rubble was visible. The volunteers held hands to form a human chain and walked across the makeshift bridge one by one.

As they reached the middle of the river, gingerly stepping over mossy rocks, the guide leading the chain stopped and signalled to the other bank. Two khaki-clad figures could be seen in the darkness. Their worst fears had come true—it was an ambush.

The human chain froze. The enemy could pick them off individually from just a few metres away, and if even one bullet found its mark and a single person fell, it would cause the whole chain to collapse into the water. How many would survive the flow was anybody's guess but the odds were not in their favour. Everyone stood absolutely still for ten minutes, expecting the first bullet to hit any moment. Meanwhile, the water level began to rise and Phadke, the shortest in the chain, could feel it creeping up at alarming speed. Standing with their rifles and ammunition held high above their heads, many of the men were beginning to lose their footing. Finally Phadke decided there was no option but to keep walking.

'If we are going to die anyway, let's at least die trying,' he shouted to Kajrekar and signalled to the guide to continue walking onward.

As they inched closer to the other bank, there was a tense silence. But then, as they scrambled up the bank from the slippery rubble, there was a sudden realisation, followed by laughter. The two 'Portuguese policemen' were tree trunks!

They huddled together for a hurried conference on the riverbank. Silvassa's eerie calm had unnerved them, and they were becoming increasingly aware of their vulnerability. They could so easily be captured or killed if the Portuguese set up an ambush. Attacking Silvassa on their own seemed foolhardy, to say the least. So they decided to wait for reinforcements.

Differences arose over what to do next. Phadke, who had been to the area with Jayantibhai Desai in his car, knew the importance of the Pipariya bridge and suggested they walk up along the river, attack Pipariya and wait there for reinforcements. Kajrekar, on the other hand, thought it was too risky to go up against twenty policemen and suggested going back to Naroli and returning the following day. Ultimately, he prevailed and they decided to head towards Naroli. However, the water level of the Daman Ganga had risen so much that the rocks they had stepped over earlier were no longer visible. With no other viable alternative, they turned towards Pipariya, determined to capture it or perish in the attempt.

The march to Pipariya was not without risk. The Phalandi stood between them and the police post. When Phadke first came here, it had been a creek a few feet across and hardly a foot deep. Now, it was gushing at great speed to meet the Daman Ganga. Though hardly waist-deep, the swift current meant they were in danger of losing their footing and being swept into the Daman Ganga just a few metres away. Left with no option, they raised their weapons above their heads and carefully stepped into the water. With everyone focused on their footing, no one noticed when Phadke lost his balance and topple headfirst into the stream. Gasping and choking, he lost his grip on the rifle as the current began to pull him towards the Daman Ganga. His head was underwater and he could not yell out for help. Fortunately, Pilaji Jadhav saw him then and, jumping into the stream, held on tight as two others lifted Phadke and pulled his waterlogged gumboots off. The river claimed his rifle and ammunition, but Phadke survived.[165]

It took them an hour to reach the Pipariya police post. A delightful sight greeted them as they crept up to the post and looked inside cautiously. Five guards, one of them clutching his bandaged side, lay tied up on the floor. They knew instantly that their teammates had already liberated Pipariya. Their full-throated cries were met with whoops of joy from near the bridge.[166]

After escorting the prisoners across the border, the two groups united and settled down in the shrubs on either side of the bridge, determined not to let anyone cross.[167]

At dawn, a few hundred metres away, across the border in Indian territory, crowds gathered. The locals had heard the shouts and slogans and guessed what had happened. Two of them detached themselves from the group and ran towards the post. It was Jayantibhai Desai, accompanied by Vasant Zanzale, who had returned from Pune.

Zanzale opened his bag and showed the group its contents: firecrackers, the kind that were colloquially referred to as 'atom bombs'. He placed one between two stones and lit the fuse. The trick they had devised while training worked

---

165 *Loksatta*, 2 August 1979.
166 Joshi, p. 69.
167 Handwritten notes by Shantaram Vaidya, sourced from his son Captain Sanjay Vaidya.

beautifully, and the resulting boom reverberated across the bridge, creating the impression of a rifle firing. The volunteers burst a few more, wanting to scare the Portuguese into thinking there were a lot of freedom fighters ready to accost them on the bridge.

Across the bridge, each little explosion added to the atmosphere of fear building up in the Portuguese camp.[168]

---

168 *Loksatta*, 2 August 1979.

Silvassa

J.R.C. Braganza, the head clerk of the forest department, was busy planning a picnic scheduled for the evening. Sub-inspectors Perreira and Noroega, along with Lobato Faria, the Patel of a few villages around Silvassa, had given him the responsibility of making the arrangements for the outing. This typically meant sending guards into the forest to steal chicken from the tribals (as well as possibly kidnap some women), picking up some liquor from the local store and arranging for a government vehicle to head out into the forest.

But the festivities scheduled for the evening of 22 July were not meant to be. At about 2 p.m., Braganza saw Lieutenant Falcao leave the police station and rush through the main square to the residence of Captain Fidaldo.

The news he carried spread quickly through the town: rebels had taken over Dadra and killed Sub-inspector Aniceto Rosario. Further, the Indian government had stopped His Excellency, the governor of Daman, from entering Dadra. Falcao and Fidaldo knew they could meet the same fate as

Rosario if they came under attack and no reinforcements were allowed to enter Nagar Haveli.

Fidaldo tried to calm everyone by telling them that Salazar, the Portuguese prime minister, was handling the situation and that everything would be brought under control very soon. However, Falcao's frequent trips between the police headquarters and Fidaldo's residence indicated the opposite. The picnic was summarily cancelled.

Very soon, the fear that was evident within the Portuguese establishment spread amongst the residents of Silvassa. They began buying and hoarding provisions, sending prices soaring by the hour.

Captain Fidaldo, once hailed as a hero following a brutal campaign he had won in Africa, was at a loss. As an emergency measure, he ordered that the Rural Guard, an auxiliary force of which Braganza was also a member, be armed and posted at Athala on the Naroli side to prevent an attack. No one was assigned to the Pipariya road because the news was that the liberators were advancing from Naroli. As mentioned earlier, Falcao had already withdrawn fifteen policemen from Pipariya to reinforce the main garrison at Silvassa.

The guards posted at Athala were ordered not to resist any intruders but to keep an eye on them. Salazar, they were told, would sort things out within a day or two.

However, the governor, speaking on Radio Daman, announced on 25 July that the orders issued by Fidaldo and Falcao stood reversed. He commanded the sipahis of the Royal Guard and the Patels to resist the 'invaders' and promised them extra remuneration for their efforts. The forces were put on full alert for three days and morale seemed to be improving when an informer brought news of the fall of Naroli. Fidaldo tried contacting Naroli to verify the news but he could not get through because the telephone lines had been cut. Panic soared again and Fidaldo posted armed guards around his residence. On 31 July, the situation became even more critical as telephones stopped working even within the town. Silvassa knew it lay isolated.

Special prayers were held in the church that evening, and emergency medical aid posts were set up in the main square. To raise morale, a church event was organised on 1 August. At 7 a.m., as citizens dressed in their Sunday best were taking the Holy Communion, shots were heard. A constable rushed in, panting, to tell them that Pipariya had fallen. The enemy was at their doorstep.

There was pandemonium. The civilians rushed for the safety of their homes, while the policemen, not knowing what to do next, milled about awaiting instructions. Fidaldo, his face ashen, shepherded his wife and daughter home. Falcao passed orders to load all weapons and position the machine guns behind the sandbags.[169]

On the same day, at about 1 p.m. Vaidya, Sinari, Zanzale, Phadke, Kajrekar and the others crouched near the Pipariya bridge, determined to hold it till the reinforcements led by Wakankar and Karmalkar reached them. They were also anticipating the arrival of the group led by Lawande. The constant lashings of rain had left them drenched and dog-tired. They had eaten only half a roti with raw onions the previous night each, supplemented by cups of tea supplied by a helpful villager. As Vaidya was not a tea drinker, he had only drunk a glass of water. He turned to Punde now and

---

169 C.R. Braganza, *Brief History of Liberation of Dadra and Nagar Haveli*, Souvenir Golden Jubilee Celebrations, 1998, pp. 58–60.

asked him to cross over to the other side and ask Phadke if he had anything to eat.[170] Just as Punde got up to do so, Vaidya pulled him back; he had heard a series of short, sharp whistles from the other side of the road.

The volunteers had decided on simple whistle-based codes before dividing themselves into two groups earlier in the morning. A long whistle meant all was clear. A series of short whistles would indicate that someone was approaching and a series of long whistles would signify an emergency.[171]

A moment later, they saw a villager on a bicycle approaching the bridge from the Silvassa side. Soon, another cyclist joined him. Both men looked nervous and were glancing left and right. Vaidya noticed that their bicycles looked new. He waited till they had reached the middle of the bridge before firing a shot at a point between them. The men panicked and fell off their bicycles. Dropping the act, they scrambled back towards the Portuguese side as the volunteers raced after them. They managed to catch one while the other disappeared into the undergrowth. Interrogating the captured cyclist revealed that they were constables of the Portuguese police who had been sent in disguise to scope out the road ahead. Obviously, some vital movement was expected on the Silvassa–Pipariya road.[172]

Now on full alert, the volunteers waited in tense anticipation, expecting a counter-attack. Though the border was just a few hundred meters away, they knew that retreat was out of the question. If they lost control of this vantage

---

170 Handwritten notes by Shantaram Vaidya, sourced from his son Captain Sanjay Vaidya.

171 Mandke, p. 41.

172 Karanjgaokar, p. 87.

point, entering Silvassa would become twice as tricky, if not impossible.

Before they could question the constable any further, they heard the sound of an approaching vehicle. There was no time to figure out who or what it could be, so the volunteers dived back into their hiding positions, dragging their prisoner with them.

The sound indicated it was a large vehicle being driven at high speed. Within minutes, they saw a station wagon approaching the bridge. The volunteers braced themselves for a hail of bullets. They knew that once the vehicle entered the police post, their cause was lost. Out of sheer desperation and in a fantastic show of marksmanship, Vaidya fired a shot, aiming for the front tyre of the station wagon. The wagon screeched to a stop and the volunteers jumped out of their hiding places and swarmed around it with their weapons drawn.[173]

Expecting to be confronted by a rain of bullets, they found that their fears were unjustified. The car had four occupants: a driver and a young man in his early thirties sat in the front and two European women, one elderly and one in her twenties, sat in the back. The young man, dressed in a long coat, his head covered with a Parsi-style pagri, stepped out of the station wagon even as Phadke and Sinari forced the driver out and threw him to the ground. Initially, the young man tried to brazen it out, saying they had no right to stop him. Angered by his insolence, Nana Soman pulled him away from the station wagon and roughed him up a little.

In just a few seconds, he broke down. He said his name was Cawasji Contractor, and he did business with the Portuguese government. He lived in Bombay and upon hearing of the

---

173 Joshi, p. 70.

disturbances in Silvassa, he had come to collect his family, who were holidaying there. Something about the answers did not seem to ring true, and the questioning continued, with increasing aggressiveness. Finally, the elderly lady asked them to stop and, opening her expensive-looking handbag, showed them a piece of paper.

A silence descended on the Dal volunteers. Written on the official letterhead of the Maharashtra chief minister and signed by Morarji Desai, the letter granted permission to Cawasji Contractor to escort two women out of Silvassa and take them safely to Bombay.

While the rest of them discussed the implications of the letter and how to respond to it, Vaidya noticed a passport in the woman's handbag. On thumbing through it, he discovered why an advance party had been sent to determine safety along the route and why the jeep had tried to speed past them—the older woman was Captain Fidaldo's wife and the younger one was his daughter.[174]

In the last week of July, Cawasji's father, Burjorji C. Contractor, a Bombay-based businessman with multiple connections to the Portuguese, had heard of Dadra's liberation and Aniceto Rosario's death. He had asked for a meeting with Dr Jivraj Mehta, the finance minister of Bombay State, who was very close to Morarji Desai. Mehta met him on 30 July, and they discussed the situation in Dadra and Nagar Haveli.

The reason for Mehta granting Burjorji an instant audience and Fidaldo trusting his wife and daughter to the custody of the younger Cawasji was the same—the prominent position

---

174 Karanjgaonkar, p. 88.

of the Parsis in society. The tiniest ethnic group in the country, which had migrated from Iran in the eighth century, had over the years become the most influential, contributing to society in significant ways. Dadabhai Naoroji was a founder of the Congress party and one of the original spokespersons of the Swadeshi movement. The most prominent Parsi family, the Tatas, had set up Tata Steel in 1907, Tata Oil Mills in 1917 and Tata Motors in 1945. Their charismatic head, J.R.D. Tata, laid the foundation for the first Indian airline with a solo flight from Karachi to Mumbai in 1932, and remained its chairman after nationalisation in 1953. The Tatas had also set up seminal institutions, like the Tata Institute of Sciences in 1911, the Tata Memorial Centre for Cancer Research in 1941 and the Tata Institute of Fundamental Research in 1945.

The Wadias, another Parsi family, had built the first dry dock in India in 1750 and, after attaining fame as shipbuilders, started Bombay Dyeing, a textile company, in 1897. The Godrej family, the Shapoorji Palonji family and many others were well-known across the country. The Parsis were also the biggest land-owning community in India, including in Dadra and Nagar Haveli. In the words of Mahatma Gandhi, the Parsi community were 'in numbers beneath contempt, in contribution beyond compare'.[175]

Suffice it to say that when a Parsi spoke, people in power listened.

Burjorji came from a long line of civil contractors and landowners with extensive business interests in Nagar Haveli and Mumbai. When Fidaldo reached out to him,

---

175 Coomi Kapoor, *The Tatas, Freddie Mercury & Other Bawas: An Intimate History of the Parsis*, Westland Non-Fiction, New Delhi, 2021.

he immediately requested a meeting with Mehta, and an appointment was granted the next day.

Burorji explained to Mehta that there were only three Portuguese officers in Dadra and Nagar Haveli—Fidaldo, Falcao, and his deputy, Pegado. If the Dal volunteers attacked Silvassa, there would be a battle and lives would be lost. Each life lost, he said, would be Indian and losing Indian lives for the sake of arresting three Portuguese officers was not very wise. He offered to send his son Cawasji to Silvassa to persuade the three Portuguese officers to surrender to the Indian authorities. If India offered them safe passage and obtained their submission, lives could be saved on both sides and Silvassa liberated without bloodshed.

Mehta agreed readily with this plan and arranged a meeting with the chief minister the following day. Burjorji went to see Desai accompanied by his daughter, and put forward his point of view. Finding that the chief minister was also favourably inclined towards any measure that would avoid bloodshed, he told him that he did a lot of business with the Portuguese government, was a close friend of the Fidaldo family and that they always stayed with him when they came to Bombay. Given this background, he offered the services of his son Cawasji and his daughter to execute the surrender.

On receiving Desai's assurance of safe passage to Goa for the three officers, he added a clause to the request. He informed Desai that he had received a letter from Mrs Fidaldo in June stating that she was suffering from some stomach ailment requiring surgery and that he had already applied for permission through proper channels for her treatment in Bombay. He pleaded with Desai to permit his son to bring Mrs Fidaldo to Bombay in his car purely on humanitarian grounds. Morarji agreed and said he felt no animosity towards any individual and that the fight was with the Portuguese state. He added that if the three officers also preferred to come to Bombay, they would be permitted to stay there without restrictions on their movement.

Burjorji then procured from the chief minister's private secretary a letter addressed to Nagarwala, asking him to ensure safe passage for his son and the occupants of his car across the border of Nagar Haveli. This was the letter Sinari and Karmalkar held in their hands on the Pipariya bridge on the afternoon of 2 August.[176]

Whether the peacenik stance was genuine or just a ruse to get Mrs Fidaldo safely out of Silvassa, as Nagarwala[177] later convinced Morarji Desai it was, is unknown. The fact remains that the volunteers believed they had stumbled upon an asset they could leverage to realise their dream of liberating Nagar Haveli, and they had no intention of ceding the advantage.

However, Mrs Fidaldo had one more surprise in her purse. She opened it, pulled out a copper plate and showed it to the volunteers. Engraved on it were terms of a treaty signed between the Portuguese and the Marathas in 1779 CE. As per the copper plate, Chimaji Appa, the brother of Bajirao Peshwa, had permitted Portuguese nationals to transit through Maratha territory. Cawasji and Mrs Fidaldo argued that both documents guaranteed safe passage, and the volunteers had no right to stop them.

---

176 Letter from Burjorji Contractor to Jawaharlal Nehru, 1955.

177 Jamshed Dorab Nagarwala first rose to fame when he was handpicked by none other than Sardar Patel to investigate the conspiracy behind the murder of Mahatma Gandhi. He got in touch with Morarji Desai during this period and fast became his favourite. He was the first inspector-general of Gujarat Police after its formation in 1960 and has a cricket stadium named after him in Ahmedabad.

After a short, hurried conference, Sinari, Karmalkar and Vaidya decided to press home their advantage and refused Cawasji and the women permission to proceed.

Karmalkar said to them, 'This territory is not part of the Maharashtrian state nor does it belong to the Marathas. We have won the place you are standing on from your government after waging war against them. This is our sovereign territory over which our rules apply. We are not bound to obey instructions given by anyone except our leadership. We will not let you go.'

He then drafted a letter in Portuguese for Fidaldo. It said, 'Your wife and daughter are in our custody. Surrender unconditionally, otherwise we will immediately shoot them dead.'

He handed the letter to Cawasji and sent him off on one of the bicycles to Silvassa. He was to return within an hour with a response.[178]

—

As Cawasji pedalled back over the bridge, he ruminated over the times he had visited Silvassa. Unlike the lively town that he remembered, with its overflowing church and bustling markets, he had found himself in a silent, desolate place instead. The streets were empty, the church was deserted and the markets closed. The police headquarters barricaded with sandbags radiated fear instead of power—and Fidaldo's residence was surrounded by grim-looking guards.

Cawasji contemplated over how resolute and determined the captain had been the previous day when he had arrived to escort Fidaldo's wife and daughter to safety. Even when

---

178 Purandare, Visheshank, p. 31.

the Parsi had conveyed to the captain the gist of his father's conversation with Morarji Desai and the offer of safe passage, Fidaldo had rejected it.

'I agree with the need to avoid bloodshed, particularly of the people of Nagar Haveli, who are prepared to fight for me. However, I am a veteran soldier and cannot withdraw until ordered. If I do so, I will be shot, and my family disgraced. I cannot surrender on my own. If the Indian government allows one of my officers to go to Daman and meet my superiors and, after hearing them or reading my message, they order me to do so, I surely will. Otherwise, I will fight.'

He stated magnanimously that he would not order the first shot to be fired. 'If the volunteers are peaceful, I will have them arrested, but if they resort to violence, I will have them shot.'

Now, approaching the residence of Fidaldo once more, he wondered if the man would go back on those words. But Fidaldo remained unyielding. His response indicated that he did not take the threat to his family seriously, probably doubting the volunteers' ability to follow through on their threat.

He wrote out a message for the Azad Gomantak Dal: 'I will not obey any orders not received from my superiors. I don't care if you shoot my wife. In case you do, she will die a martyr. Her bravery will be cherished and rejoiced by Portuguese subjects. Her sacrifice will always be remembered.'[179]

Cawasji handed over this response from the administrator to Karmalkar and the group went into a huddle to determine the next course of action. Fidaldo had called their bluff, knowing they would not shoot the hostages in cold blood.

---

179 Letter from Burjorji Contractor to Jawaharlal Nehru, 1955.

They decided upon a change of approach and drafted another note to the captain.

'We are marching tomorrow morning to attack you, and your wife and friends, tied to the bonnet of their station wagon, will be in the forefront. Any harm to them will be solely your responsibility.'[180]

Meanwhile, the two women sat on their luggage in the middle of the road, next to the punctured wagon, encircled by gruff Dal volunteers who were just as scared, cold and miserable. Burjorji would later complain to Nehru in a letter dated 17 January 1955 (acknowledged by the prime minister's office on 22 February 1955) that the women were ill-treated and not even offered a glass of water. Not only that, they were threatened and continuously surrounded by Dal volunteers brandishing weapons. He seemed oblivious to the fact that the volunteers themselves had not eaten for over thirty-six hours.

After sending Cawasji off to Silvassa a second time, Karmalkar escorted the women to Lavachha and handed them over to Mohan Singh Zala, the officer in charge of the police post there. Zala gave them food, offered them a place to rest and, the same evening, transferred them to Nagarwala, who sent them onward to Bombay, where Mrs Fidaldo and her daughter would take refuge in the Portuguese consulate.[181]

Meanwhile, Cawasji had returned with a response within an hour. Fidaldo had rejected their terms once again. 'I have no orders to submit, and my government has asked me to fight to the finish if you turn violent. I suggest you allow Lieutenant Falcao or me to proceed safely to Daman through Indian territory. We will explain the situation to our superiors

---

180 Joshi, p. 70.

181 Letter from Burjorji Contractor to Jawaharlal Nehru, 1955.

and obtain and carry out their orders. If they ask me to surrender, I will surrender; if they ask me to fight, I will fight. However, if you do not let either of us move out of Silvassa, I will do what I think is right for my country.'[182]

After receiving this response, the volunteers decided to wait for Wakankar and Lawande to join them before deciding on their next course of action.

On the Pipariya bridge, the bursting of crackers continued. Fidaldo had to be made to believe that a large force with adequate weaponry was about to attack Silvassa. It was psychological warfare at its best, and necessary since the actual ammunition available to them was insufficient even for an hour-long firefight. The orders from Wakankar and Lawande were clear—as far as possible, they were not to fire a single bullet till they entered Silvassa, so as to conserve their stock of ammunition.[183]

As the sun set and darkness enveloped them, neither the news that Cawasji had brought nor Fidaldo's response seemed encouraging. When quizzed by Sinari and Vaidya about the strength and level of preparedness of the Portuguese, Cawasji had informed them that their enemy had enough resources to engage them for as long as a week. He had served as a flight lieutenant in the RAF in the Second World War and warned the volunteers that, in his professional opinion, they had no

---

182 Ibid.
183 Handwritten notes by Shantaram Vaidya, sourced from his son Captain Sanjay Vaidya.

chance of either liberating Silvassa or coming back from there alive.[184]

As they crouched beneath the bridge, they knew that the next day, 2 August 1954, would be the most glorious day of their life, or the last.

The situation in Silvassa was no better. Cawasji had been unable to confirm the number of attackers present. All that the Portuguese knew was that besides the volunteers in Pipariya, there were others coming from the Naroli side, while more were amassing at Lavachha. It was also not known how well-armed they were. The continuous firing indicated they had adequate ammunition and confidence in their skills. Fidaldo and Falcao were increasingly leaning towards the notion that the so-called 'volunteers' were, as they had initially thought, Special Reserve Police jawans in civilian clothing and that the onslaught was being orchestrated by trained militia with unlimited resources and the full support of the Indian government.

As Falcao oversaw the preparations and positioned his forces, he received an urgent summons from Fidaldo, who had received a note that confirmed their worst fears. The 'volunteers' were military jawans! The message, sent through one of the policemen captured at Pipariya, was from Nagarwala, and it simply said, 'Surrender immediately, or we are coming for you tomorrow.'

Not knowing this was a part of the strategy to psyche them out, Fidaldo ordered his soldiers to abandon the barricade and assemble outside the headquarters for a briefing.

The battle lines were now drawn on both sides.

---

184 Letter from Burjorji Contractor to Jawaharlal Nehru, 1955.

Just after sunset on 1 August, Wakankar arrived in Lavachha with the last batch of volunteers from Pune. Natekar arranged hot cups of tea and a simple meal of rice and dal for everyone. The men were drenched, but in high spirits, and raring to go at this enemy they knew so little about. The total number of fighters, including those from Goa, had increased to over 125. Calling them fighters, however, was generous, considering that most of them had never handled a weapon before. In all, only twenty had had some exposure to firearms or had previously discharged one. This count included those already active in the struggle. The rest were armed with sticks, swords, knives and the occasional axe, while many had no weapons.

On hearing about Wakankar's arrival, Jayantibhai Desai met him in Lavachha and briefed him about the role of Cawasji and the various communications received from Fidaldo. Wakankar rushed to Pipariya and held an urgent meeting with the team there. The consensus was that they could negotiate a surrender if they allowed Fidaldo to communicate with his superiors in Daman. That would be preferable to exposing their mostly raw, untrained 'army' to trained Portuguese guns. Even if the final decision by the Portuguese was not to surrender, the worst that could follow was an open battle. This was an option they were prepared for anyway, and allowing Fidaldo to talk to his superiors would not compromise their current position. With this in mind, they decided to send Cawasji on one more trip to Silvassa with a note offering one of the Portuguese officers safe passage to Daman.

Cawasji had reunited with his sister in Lavachha by then. When Wakankar and a few Dal volunteers knocked on his door and asked him to proceed immediately to Silvassa, he refused. His reasons were logical. He had not slept the previous night and, having twice cycled to Silvassa in heavy rain, was feeling tired and feverish. He also feared being mistaken for an intruder by either side in the dark and getting shot. However, he agreed to go at daybreak.

At the crack of dawn, Cawasji left once more on his peace mission to Silvassa. Pedalling vigorously, he arrived at the town square in less than an hour and rushed to the administrator's house, but to his surprise, found it deserted. He searched all over town but found no trace of the Portuguese officers. The police headquarters were still barricaded and manned but inaccessible. Of course, no one fired at him from behind the sandbags because everyone knew him, but no one responded to him either when he shouted out for Fidaldo. The city lay deserted, with no one to tell him what had happened overnight. Finally, two guards posted at Falcao's house informed him that Fidaldo, Falcao and Pegado had marched out of town, accompanied by 150 men, just after he left. They had crossed the river and taken up positions, possibly to launch a counter-attack. That left less than a hundred men at the Silvassa headquarters and a few subalterns, all from Goa or Daman. There was no longer the possibility of allowing one of the officers access to Daman—attacking Silvassa was the only option.[185] Cawasji rushed back to Lavachha with the news but found that the Dal volunteers had crossed over and taken up positions within a kilometre of Silvassa. The information he had brought did not alter the dynamics—if Fidaldo was not considering surrender, they would have to attack Silvassa.

---

185 Letter from Burjorji Contractor to Jawaharlal Nehru, 1955.

Silvassa Liberated

THE leaders of each volunteer group spent the night of 1 August briefing the newcomers and assigning them specific responsibilities. They were divided into four teams of thirty each and placed under the command of Sinari, Vaidya, Wakankar and Lawande. Each squad had five volunteers with rifles and pistols and a certain number of men who were armed with swords and axes. Those with no weapons at all were given the 'atom bombs' and told to burst them when signalled as well as shout slogans and create a lot of noise to give the impression of a sizeable army marching in (and to do so while staying out of range of the Portuguese guns). The plan was to approach the Silvassa police headquarters from four directions, bursting crackers and making enough noise to intimidate the Portuguese.

By 8 a.m., the teams left their hiding places and set off on the march to Silvassa, keeping off the road and moving swiftly beneath the trees, occasionally stopping to take shelter in a house. Only the station wagon, with Mrs

Fidaldo supposedly in it, drove on the main road parallel to the marching convoys—the loud bursting of crackers and shouting of slogans continued till they reached close to the town square.[186]

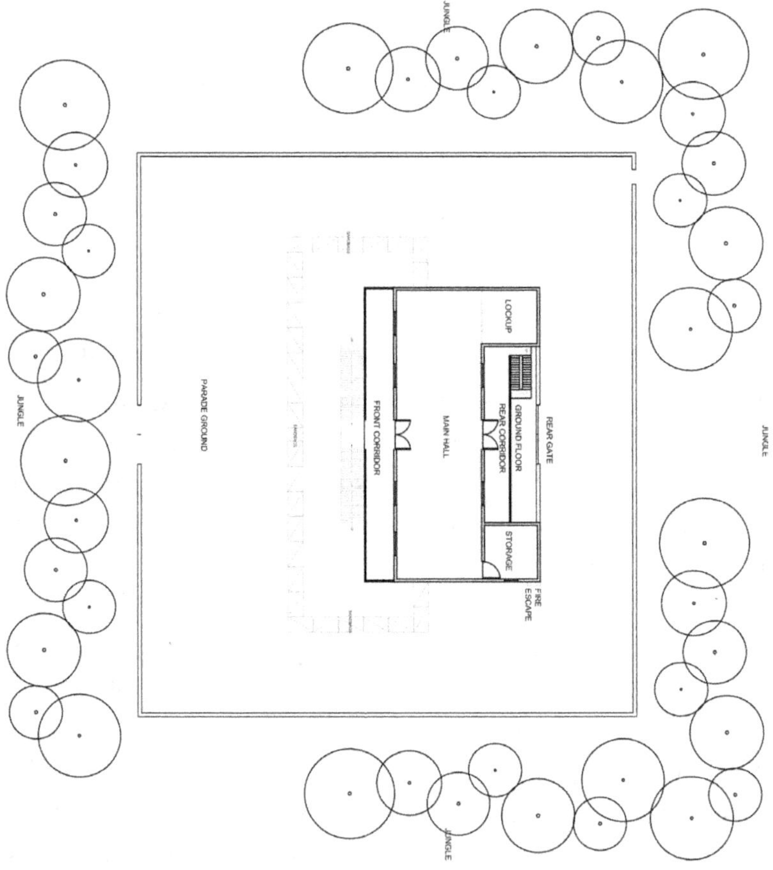

Conceptual plan of the police post in Silvassa, based on descriptions provided by volunteers

The senior members of the group were familiar with the appearance of the building since they had seen the pictures

---

186 Handwritten notes by Shantaram Vaidya, sourced from his son Captain Sanjay Vaidya.

taken by Lalita Phadke. To the rank and file, though, it looked quite foreboding. The dusty square, the Portuguese flag fluttering atop a flag post in the middle and a massive wall of sandbags, above which part of the roof was visible. Scarier still was the sight of rifles and Sten guns jutting out through small slits between the sandbags. It was clear that storming the building from the front was not a good idea since anyone entering the square would come directly into the line of fire. Anyway, the plan was to get to the terrace and drop down to the first-floor balcony at the rear of the building. They would engage the guards there while one or two men rushed down the staircase to open the backdoor and let the others in.[187]

The three groups led by Sinari, Lawande and Wakankar crept forward from three sides, ensuring they stayed out of range of the rifles, while a fourth, led by Vaidya, made its way to the rear. This team, which included Pilaji Jadhav, Bhopale, Shivram Thuse and eight others, was best equipped to enter the building since Vaidya and Jadhav had already been inside once, during their recce disguised as beggars.[188] They knew the only way to the terrace was via a rusty fire escape. Much to their relief, they found it unguarded. Ascending stealthily, they reached the terrace from where they could peer down at the rear balcony. Eight or ten guards were stationed below, their attention focused on the room at the front.[189]

Vaidya waved a scrap of white cloth at the Wakankar group and waited for the action to begin. At Wakanker's signal, all three groups started firing, bursting crackers and yelling slogans. Seeing the guards stiffen and aim their weapons

---

187 Joshi, p. 71.

188 Handwritten notes by Shantaram Vaidya, sourced from his son Captain Sanjay Vaidya.

189 Ibid.

towards the front, Vaidya commanded Thuse to jump into the verandah. Thuse did so, followed by the rest.

Unfortunately, Thuse misjudged the distance, fell on a chair and landed on his back. A policeman, alerted by the sound, turned and aimed his bayonet at Thuse's chest. Bhopale, who had landed on his feet, swung his axe and severed the policeman's hand at the elbow. Vasant Badwe, who jumped in next, also landed poorly. When another policeman rushed towards him, Vaidya, who had leapt in as well, thrust his bayonet into his ribcage. The policeman fell to the floor, bleeding profusely. As the remaining policemen turned to attack, Vaidya fired, and two collapsed to the floor.

Meanwhile, one of the volunteers had run down the staircase and opened the back door. Around thirty-five volunteers led by Wakankar raced in, brandishing their weapons. Seeing themselves grossly outnumbered, the remaining policemen in the back verandah surrendered. Leaving a few men behind to guard them, the volunteers then raced to the front of the building and shouted at the policemen there to lay down their arms. Two attempted to fire their guns but were bayoneted, and collapsed. Taken entirely by surprise, both by the direction of the attack and its ferociousness, the remaining Portuguese soldiers in the room surrendered. By this time, the volunteers in the front had stormed the sandbagged building and captured the policemen who were posted there. The battle for Silvassa was over within minutes.

Victory slogans and whoops of joy rent the air. Wakankar took charge and lined up the arrested policemen in two groups under a tree opposite the headquarters.[190] A head count showed that there were fifty-five of them, including five subalterns. Most of them were locals, and the rest from

---

190 Joshi, p. 72.

Daman or Goa. With their officers gone, morale was low and surrender seemed the best option.

Dhanaji Burungale then went up the flag pole, removed the Portuguese flag and threw it down. It was such a cathartic moment for the Dal volunteers that some began to stomp and dance on it. Bindu Madhav Joshi, at twenty-six, probably one of the oldest in the group, rushed to stop them. 'It is not just a piece of cloth,' he said, gesturing at the flag. 'It is a symbol of our victory. Let us not destroy it.'

The voice of reason prevailed, and the flag was folded and kept away carefully inside the building. It was later presented to Morarji Desai, before being handed over to Bindu Madhav Joshi for safekeeping.[191]

The tricolour was brought out in a solemn ceremony, and there was pin-drop silence as Shamrao Lad and Atmaram Mayekar marched to the flagstaff to hoist it. That was when a bullet hit Lad.

The crack of the rifle was loud enough to be heard all over town. Lad fell, as did Mayekar, both bleeding profusely. Vidyadhar Tilak, another volunteer who was standing near the flagpole, screamed and collapsed. Sinari and a few other men dashed in the direction from which the bullet had come, weapons drawn. They found a Portuguese constable with his hands raised in the air, fear writ large on his face, begging for mercy. He had forgotten to lock the safety catch, and the bullet had escaped his rifle accidentally. It had hit the concrete base of the flagstaff, causing splinters to fly in all directions. While one injured Mayekar in the thigh, another had pierced the eye of Lad. The main body of the bullet itself had ricocheted

---

191 The flag then passed into the custody of Moreshwar Purandare, who displayed it in a glass case in the drawing room of his Pune house, where it remains today.

off the base and hit Vidhyadhar Tilak. Understanding the situation, Sinari managed to calm the furious Dal volunteers down, explaining that it had been a mistake. A lynching was averted.

Dr Kashinath Sanzgiri, the doctor accompanying the volunteers, administered first aid and sent all three off to Bombay for further treatment. While the other two recovered, Lad sadly lost his right eye.[192]

While this was going on, a jeep came roaring in. It screeched to a halt, and a short, slim man dressed in battle fatigues ran out and embraced Wakankar. It was Phadke, who had stayed back at Pipariya to receive Vinayakrao Apte of the RSS, who had insisted on being the first on the spot after the liberation. Amidst more sloganeering, on 2 August at 2 p.m.,[193] the tricolour was finally raised on the flag pole at Silvassa, in the spot where the Portuguese flag had fluttered for 187 years.

Volunteers took down the picture of Salazar on the wall of the police headquarters. There was, however, nothing to replace it with as portraits of Indian leaders as well as Indian deities were banned in Portuguese territories. Rummaging through the stationary in the police station, one of the volunteers discovered a picture of Krishna on the inside cover of an exercise book. He put this up in place of Salazar's image, and with that, the battle for Silvassa was over.[194]

The war, however, was not yet won. Fidaldo, Falcao and Pegado were nowhere to be seen. Though the prisoners had indicated that the three had marched out of Silvassa with their most trained and experienced men, the possibility of

---

192　Lawande, p. 217.

193　Joshi, p. 77.

194　*Hindustan Times*, 2 August 1954.

this being a trap was real. With the officers at large, the fear of a counter-attack loomed.

The local population was too shell-shocked to emerge onto the streets. An eerie silence prevailed across Silvassa. The volunteers immediately launched a search operation to eliminate the possibility of the Portuguese officials hiding somewhere in the town.[195] A group led by Shrikrishna Bhide moved from door to door. They took the help of police constables Rajendra and Kashinath Desai, who pointed out the houses of the Portuguese sympathisers, which they then entered and searched thoroughly. They questioned the residents and confiscated a few weapons but found no trace of the Portuguese officers.

In one of the lanes leading off the main square, they came upon a few houses that were, without exception, occupied only by older men or children—all the able-bodied men and the women were missing. On intense questioning, one of the older men told them that the women were hiding in a house at the end of the street.

Volunteers surrounded the house, which had a raised open courtyard in the front and a roof-high wooden door set into a stone wall. When knocking on it did not yield results, they fired into the air and banged on it again. An old man opened the door, looking frightened. Bhide told him they wanted to search the house and meet every person inside, including the women.

Under threat of being arrested and maybe shot, the older man called the women out one by one. Though Bhide assured them they were safe, the women were shaking with fright, certain that this decency was just a charade. Bhide stood near the main gate, looked at each woman as she came out

---

195 Mandke, p. 46.

and waved her to one side of the courtyard. After everyone had emerged, the volunteers searched the house, but found nothing.

Before they left, Bhide addressed them. 'We have the utmost respect for all women and consider you like our mother and sisters. What we did was our duty and if, in the process, we have hurt anyone's sentiments, we sincerely apologise. To ensure your safety, we will post some of our volunteers outside this house. If you feel unsafe, feel free to call us.'

Hearing this, two older women stepped forward with folded hands. 'All of us here are the wives, daughters or daughters-in-law of prominent citizens of Silvassa. Our men are either in hiding or out of Nagar Haveli. We were misguided about you and told that you were looters and barbarians. We feel completely safe now and will tell our men not to fear you.'

Some of the women were tearful with relief and insisted that the volunteers step in to eat something. Bhide politely refused, saying that there were many others waiting in the town square who were also very hungry and he would prefer to return and eat with them.

The news of their gentlemanly behaviour spread like wildfire. The following day, when volunteers stood on guard duty outside the police headquarters, people filed past them, smiling, greeting them, and even saluting. 'Bharat mata ki jai!' was a common refrain in the town hall of Silvassa for many days after.[196]

---

196 Joshi, p. 75.

While the search operations were ongoing, Wakankar worked on consolidating the gains from the attack. To streamline the administrative processes, he sent volunteers to fetch the parish priest, the public prosecutor and the postmaster, the three prominent members of the Portuguese establishment who remained in town after the departure of Fidaldo and the others.

Suspecting that the Portuguese might be hiding in the local church, Joshi, Thuse, Punde and three others were despatched to search the premises and bring the parish priest to the headquarters.

Built in 1897, Our Lady of Piety Church[197] was one of the major landmarks of Silvassa. A Gothic structure made of grim, grey stone, it made for an arresting sight with its colourful stained-glass windows and huge doors on both sides of the altar. The church bells hung from a turret-like tower attached to the roof of another building abutting the main hall. The overall effect was of an imposing structure, one with many nooks and crannies where a man could hide.

The team led by Thuse jumped over the stone wall and spread out on all sides to encircle the structure. Zigzagging to the main building of the church, they were met with no resistance. The church was empty. The magnificent altar, the pews and a copy of *The Last Supper* stared back at them. After reassuring themselves that there was nobody there, they opened the main door and began searching the premises. They found the priest hiding behind the altar. Joshi politely requested his permission to search the place and asked him to come with them. The priest was initially hesitant but then

---

197 The church still stands in all its magnificence opposite the tribal museum in Silvassa. Visitors come to admire the scene of the last supper painted on its ceiling. It is said to be modelled on the Sagrada church in Barcelona designed by Antoni Gaudi.

agreed, asking only that he be given some time to pray before leaving the church.

Joshi and his men stepped outside the church to wait for the priest. Suddenly, the loud chiming of church bells reverberated through the town square. The priest had rushed into the adjoining building, locked it from inside, and run up to the terrace to ring the twin brass bells. It was unclear to Joshi whether this was a signal to attack or for people to gather in the church. Regardless, he and Punde ran to the belfry, dragged the priest away from the bells and frog-marched him to the police headquarters.[198]

To summon the public prosecutor, Wakankar had sent Ganesh Joglekar. 'I am sure he speaks English,' he said, referring to the prosecutor. 'And you speak it best amongst us. Request him to come, but if he refuses, get him anyway.' He assigned four armed volunteers to accompany Joglekar and handed him a loaded pistol.

The prosecutor lived in a single-storey stone house set amidst a large garden; the doors were locked and the windows barred. As Joglekar opened the outer gate, one of the volunteers stopped him and gestured that he should stand back. Then the two of them opened fire with their rifles, and the bullets bounced off the stone walls, creating a ruckus. After two minutes of firing, they gestured at Joglekar to proceed. When Joglekar knocked on the door, a middle-aged man opened it, trembling.

'Do you welcome us here?' Joglekar asked the man, who responded with a hesitant yes.

'Where are they?' the man asked, referring to Fidaldo, Falcao and Pegado.

---

198 Karanjgaonkar, p. 97.

'In our custody,' replied Joglekar. 'Don't be afraid of us. We are the Azad Gomantak Dal and we want your cooperation. I have to take you to our commander. Come with us.'

Before he could respond, a loud wail hit their ears. The man's wife, standing behind the bedroom door, had burst out crying.

'Go and tell her not to worry,' Joglekar said, exasperated. The man entered the bedroom and closed the door behind him. A moment later, Joglekar heard a drawer open. He ran to the room and kicked the door open. The prosecutor was taking a pistol out of the drawer. Joglekar lunged forward, snatched it from him and held his own gun against the man's head. Once he had been subdued, he was marched off to meet Wakankar.[199]

Unlike the others, the postmaster came without a fuss but insisted on sprouting a lot of legalese about how he was not bound to obey the orders of anyone but the government. On being firmly told that the Azad Gomantak Dal was now the government, he sullenly agreed to cooperate.[200]

The first communication sent out from the post office under the new regime was a two-word telegram from Phadke. Addressed to Lata Mangeshkar, it simply said: 'Silvassa liberated.'[201]

—

Lawande and Wakankar now took charge of the offices and the treasury in the presence of the postmaster and the public prosecutor. As the keys to the central safe couldn't be found, a

199 *Dainik Tarun Bharat*, 2 August 1979.
200 Joshi, p. 73.
201 In conversation with Shreedhar Phadke.

volunteer broke the lock by hitting it with the butt of a revolver. They found ₹1,15,000 in the safe, besides 20,000 escudos, the Portuguese currency. These were carefully counted and stored away. From the state of the safe, it was clear it had held more and that someone had hurriedly removed the cash.

As they were emptying the safe, a cloth-bound package fell out. When they saw it contents, everyone burst out laughing. They were arrest warrants for Lawande, Sinari, Waz, Bhikubhai Pandya and Vaman Desai. There were photographs of each of them, and detailed descriptions. They had been declared enemies of the state. Ironically, the enemies of the state had now become the state.

Police uniforms, bicycles, numerous registers and knives were also found in the building and stored away.

A search of Fidaldo's house resulted in the discovery of twenty leather bags full of expensive clothes and jewellery. These were also deposited in the treasury.[202]

The armoury yielded 275 bayonets, thirty-five Lee Enfield rifles, twenty-three revolvers, three 12 Bore pump action guns and three Sten guns besides twenty-eight cartons of ammunition, each bearing 1,000 bullets. There was no trace of the machine guns, and there was just one carbine which, on testing, was found to be not operational. In addition, numerous empty cartons of ammunition lay strewn about. It was clear that the Portuguese had retreated with the best weapons.[203]

—

That same afternoon, Lawande took over as administrator of the liberated territories and issued several proclamations.

---

202 Lawande, p. 219.
203 Joshi, p. 77.

He directed the town crier to announce the news of recent developments all over Silvassa, asking people to cooperate with the new administration and assuring them that no one would be harmed. It was also announced that if anyone was sheltering or helping the three fugitive Portuguese officers, they would be arrested or even shot. All those who owned firearms were commanded to deposit them with the administration.[204]

Lawande also held a press conference, which he and Karmalkar jointly addressed. They announced the ouster of the Portuguese and the taking over of the administration by the Azad Gomantak Dal. The national press covered the event widely, and there were questions about the future course of action. This was not something Karmalkar and Lawande could shed light on. They had been focused on executing the plan to expel the Portuguese, not on what they would do afterwards. Their responses to questions about how they would administer the territories were vague and unclear. A question about how they planned to dislodge the forces of Fidaldo was met with a particularly interesting non-sequitur. A reporter asked the question of Karmalkar, who quickly passed it on to Kajrekar.

'I am not yet married,' responded Kajrekar.

When pressed to explain this strange answer, he said, 'Had I been married, I wouldn't have shared the plan even with my wife, so the question of sharing it with you does not arise.' The response, evasive and confusing, did little to conceal the lack of a vision.[205]

Some disagreements between the various groups operating under the umbrella of the Dal also surfaced. There was

---

204 Lawande, p. 219.
205 Kajrekar, p. 44.

dissatisfaction about not having been consulted about the press statements.[206] But the euphoria of victory papered these over temporarily, and anyway, the challenge of defeating the Fidaldo-led strike force was more urgent for the moment.

At the press conference, Wakankar paraded the prisoners they had taken and told the assembled gathering that there was no danger to them from the Dal. As long as they were loyal to the new regime, they could carry on as before. There was wild cheering at this news, for the locals had been apprehensive about their fate.

The most insightful comment that evening came from Mohan Ranade, who was on guard duty along with another Dal worker, Anant Thali.

'Look at them, Anant,' he said. 'See how they have changed their hats? Till yesterday, they were praising the Portuguese, and if they had known about us, most of them would have got us arrested. Today, they are shouting our slogans with us, even saluting and thanking us.'[207]

The night of 2 August passed relatively peacefully as the Daman Ganga continued to overflow, making it unlikely that the Portuguese would return. As a precaution, some volunteers took up guard duty at the police headquarters and others positioned themselves near the river. Most of them were fatigued and in need of rest, but the heady excitement of victory kept them awake.

The next day, two problems of another kind arose.

In the morning, Wakankar received an urgent summons from Nagarwala. When they met, he was informed by

---

206 Ranade, p. 39.
207 Ibid.

a furious Nagarwala that some of the Dal volunteers had stolen cash and jewellery from the central safe. Names of the possible suspects had been provided to him by some members of the Dal who had thought it appropriate to inform him rather than the Dal leadership, not knowing how deep the malaise was. Wakankar, of course, was furious too and, upon returning, raised such a hue and cry that the person who had stolen the jewellery quietly brought it back.[208] As for the cash, the thief offered the flimsy excuse that he had taken it for the Dal's expenses. Since Wakankar did not reveal the person's name, the Pune and the Goa groups began to suspect and blame each other. From then on, Sane, Zanzale and Vaidya, all from Pune, guarded the treasury while Bhatt and Naik, who were from Goa, monitored all disbursements. Since members of both groups were made accountable, the controversy was put to rest.[209]

The second crisis arose with the arrival of thirty more volunteers from Pune. During the mobilisation in Pune, Wakankar had contacted many groups, most of whom responded positively. Not all of them were able to join the first batch, however, and many had left a day or two after, arriving after the battle for Silvassa. Most of them were college students, who arrived in high spirits, blood pumping with adrenaline. In a charged-up state, they roved the streets of Silvassa and, mistaking some of the residents' Christian and Goan names for Portuguese ones, turned their hatred on them. Barging into offices and houses, they ransacked

---

208 Though many have hazarded guesses about who the thief was, with both the Pune and Goa volunteers blaming someone from the opposite camp, there was no reference to the name in any of the documents studied. It is a secret that has remained firmly with Wakankar and Nagarwala.

209 Parshuram Sane, *Smritigandh*, p. 34.

the rooms and even vandalised the altars and crosses on the premises. In a single hour, all the goodwill the Dal had earned vanished into thin air.

The leaders took this very seriously. Lawande dispatched a team to detain the newcomers and discipline them. He also called an urgent meeting attended by Sinari, Wakankar, Zanzale, Phadke and Karmalkar. They agreed unanimously that the movement would be weakened if painted in a communal hue. All of the newcomers were immediately packed off to Pune. The firm handling of a potentially explosive situation earned them appreciation not only in Silvassa but also from Morarji Desai.[210]

The challenge now was to figure out the next phase of the battle.

---

210 Lawande, p. 221.

Wrath of the Warlis

WHEN 200 members of the Portuguese force lined up outside the police headquarters just before the attack on 1 August, they had no idea what was coming. Because Fidaldo had been inspecting their positions and joking with them just a while ago, they were justified in thinking that he wished to brief them on defence strategy or give them a pep talk. Instead, he asked most of them to prepare to leave. Those who were to remain were instructed to resist for as long as they could, and if arrested, to not try and escape.

Over 150 of the best-trained men in the Portuguese force marched out from Silvassa within an hour with the most superior firearms available at the headquarters, as well as ammunition and cash. It was clear to those left behind that they were not conducting a tactical retreat but leaving to never return.

The policemen under Fidaldo crossed the Daman Ganga and stopped on the opposite bank, intending to observe what went on and plan a counteroffensive. But it was raining heavily, and the water levels rose rapidly until the river was in full spate. Wisely, Fidaldo decided it would be safer to take a stand elsewhere.

In the heavy rain and pitch darkness, the force marched past the cemetery, heading for the forest of Sailli. Walking through slush with zero visibility, some fell into the shallow, unprotected wells (known as viris) along the way and had to be pulled out. A few discarded their heavy ammunition bags and threw away their shoes, which kept getting stuck in the mud. Others deserted ranks and abandoned the march, heading back to their villages. After losing their way numerous times, the group finally reached Sailli and rested in the abandoned huts of the Warlis. The entire village was empty, so they presumed the Warlis had fled into the jungle on seeing them.

At 4 a.m., they left Sailli and marched to Rakholi. Arriving at the river bank, they stopped at the house of a well-known moneylender and trader whom later records refer to as the Brahmin of Rakholi. He offered them tea and food. At about noon, when they heard gunshots from the direction of Silvassa, they understood it had been lost. There was nothing to be done now but forge ahead.

Before they could absorb the implications of the loss, at about 3 p.m., they received a message from across the river: surrender or die. The messenger warned Fidaldo that 4,000 Warlis had gathered on the other side of the river, at Vasona, armed with pellet guns, machetes, knives and swords, ready to strike them down if they crossed the river. Now, the men could not head back to Silvassa as the Azad Gomantak Dal controlled it, and they could not move forward because of the Warlis.

Fidado refused to respond to the threat, perhaps because the Portuguese had always been dismissive of the Warlis and did not think they would dare to challenge them in an open fight. The silence seemed to embolden the Warlis, and cries of 'Fanagache Raj vaun geulo' (the river has washed away the Portuguese Raj) could be heard. Preferring to fight the Warlis rather than the Dal, which he still presumed comprised trained members of the Special Reserve Police, Fidaldo ordered his troops to fire across the river. Rather than intimidating them, the shots seemed to inflame the Warlis, and they fired back. The return fire seriously injured two Portuguese constables. Fidaldo then ordered his troops to set up the machine guns. As the steady *rat-a-tat* of the guns echoed through the forest, the return fire slowed noticeably. The machine-gun posts were well protected, and the Portuguese suffered no further damage, but the moans and cries from across the river confirmed that the Warlis had taken hits. After approximately two hours of this, the firing from the Warli side suddenly ceased. Either due to a lack of firepower or the fear of the Portuguese that was still embedded in their hearts, the Warlis withdrew into the jungle, their resistance seemingly at an end.[211]

On the morning of 3 August, Fidaldo checked the water level in the Daman Ganga and figured they could cross the river. They marched without a pause until they reached Dapada. Covering a distance of five kilometres in a little over an hour, they got to the police outpost there, but found it abandoned and smouldering. The Warlis had attacked it and set it on fire, making a bonfire of the revenue records, which the landlords used to keep them enslaved.[212]

---

211 C.R. Braganza, *Brief History of Liberation of Dadra and Nagar Haveli*, Souvenir Golden Jubilee Celebrations, 1998, pp. 61–62.
212 Prabhakar Vaidya, *Nagar Havelicha Muktisangram Anee Mee*, Rajamal Prakashan, Goa, 1981, p. 19–20.

Hungry and tired, the men found nothing to meet their needs and had to be satisfied with quenching their thirst at a stream. By now, they had marched about twelve kilometres through the sludge in the pouring rain and had not eaten a proper meal for over thirty-six hours. What kept them going was the depressing knowledge that they had very few options and the hope that they would find the Khadoli distillery open.[213]

The distillery was owned by the Keni family from Goa, who manufactured liquor from jaggery and supplied it to the Portuguese officers and their staff. It was equidistant from Dapada and Khanvel, about five kilometres each way. Fidaldo and his officers decided to dig in and take a stand at either of these places. Both had the same advantage—proximity to Warli villages from where chicken and the occasional goat could be seized, as well as to the distillery where liquor was abundantly available. Fidaldo calculated that if he could hole up long enough at Khanvel, there would be time for reinforcements to arrive from Daman. Alternatively, international pressure might cause the Indians to withdraw or seek some middle path. Either situation would save him from potential embarrassment. But most urgently, his troops needed food and drink, and the distillery was the perfect spot to get both.

However, Fidaldo's calculations once again failed to account for the Warlis' wrath. The tired and hungry forces reached the distillery by evening and witnessed complete chaos. The compound wall had a gaping hole and the huge iron gate creaked ominously on damaged hinges. The smashed

---

213 C.R. Braganza, *Brief History of Liberation of Dadra and Nagar Haveli*, Souvenir Golden Jubilee Celebrations, 1998, pp. 58–60.

remnants of liquor bottles were strewn all over the floor, and the doors and window were shattered. On seeing them, the frightened workers emerged from their hiding places to tell them what had happened. A group of Warlis led by lal baotas (communists) had broken into the distillery and beaten the guards and workers. They had seized all the liquor, destroying what they could not carry.

Fidaldo told the workers that he was in control now and assured them that he and his men would be camping at Khanvel, just five kilometres away. They could call for help any time they felt threatened. In return, and this went without saying, they would have to provide his men with food and drink.

After spending two rather pleasant days in Khadoli, the men marched into Khanvel, only to find it deserted.[214] There were a few people in the patelado (administrative) building next to the police station, where they also found the families of Menezes and Lobato Faria, the two Patels of the area, hiding in the cellar. The Warlis had struck again. Fidaldo was informed that, led by the lal baotas, they had torn through the station, driving away the few policemen present, and occupied the building. However, upon hearing the sound of the Portuguese forces marching in, they had panicked and fled into the jungle.[215] News of the losses in the river battle at Rakholi had possibly reached them, and they must have feared they would meet the same fate.

His confidence bolstered by this and the easy availability of liquor, Fidaldo ordered his troops to set up camp and secure the premises. Since the police station was not large enough to

---

214 Sinari, p. 119, and an interview with Deepak Jadhav.

215 C.R. Braganza, *Brief History of Liberation of Dadra and Nagar Haveli*, Souvenir Golden Jubilee Celebrations, 1998, pp. 60–62.

host all of them, they also took over the patelado next door and set up sandbag fortifications. This time, he ensured that the sandbags surrounded the station and the patelado, leaving no gap for the Dal volunteers to breach. He had enough manpower, ammunition, food and drink, and the buildings were located at a height, allowing them to observe and shoot down anyone who approached, so he felt perfectly safe.[216]

---

216 Vaidya, p. 48.

Recalibration

THE rain did not stop for the next two days. Wakankar, Kajrekar, Phadke, Shantaram Vaidya, Bhopale, Jadhav and a few others from Pune, and Sinari, Lawande, Bhatt and Karmalkar from Goa were among those who were cooped up in Silvassa during this period. Prabhakar Vaidya, a college student from Pune, was a notable addition to the team. Originally from Kunkalli in Goa, he was a football player and athlete who had known Sinari and Lawande during his time in Goa. On hearing of the liberation of Silvassa and the stories of bravery that had begun circulating in Pune, he skipped a college tournament and boarded a train to Vapi to meet Sinari and congratulate him, fully intending to return to college the next day. But the tales about the battle excited him so much that he decided to stay on. As it turned out, he would play a crucial role in subsequent events.[217]

---

217 Vaidya, p. 5-6.

The original plan floated by Sinari was to trap the Portuguese in Rakholi before they could cross the river. He set off on a reconnaissance mission with a few others on the evening of 3 August, and found the river in full spate. The area where the Portuguese were said to be camping lay in total darkness. So, he returned to recalibrate his plan.[218]

On 6 August, Wakankar and Prabhakar Vaidya decided to learn more about the camp. Since getting there unnoticed was not feasible in the daytime, they sought the help of some Warlis from a village near Silvassa to gather information. The Warlis returned in the evening with the news that the Portuguese troops had crossed the river and gone on to either Dapada or Khanvel.

Vaidya and Wakankar decided to go looking for any stragglers who may have fallen behind. It was important to arrest them and bring them back to Silvassa, they felt. Along with the Desai brothers and a few other men, they commandeered a jeep and left for Rakholi at 5 p.m. They drove slowly and carefully, alert for ambushes along the way. About a kilometre away from Rakholi, they came across a Warli man walking along the side of the road with his son. He tried to run into the bushes at the sight of the armed men in the jeep, but when they assured him that they had no intention of harming either him or his son, he told them that most of the Portuguese had already crossed over but that a few had probably stayed back. He pointed out the house of the brahmin moneylender where they had camped.

Wakankar parked the jeep a few metres from the house and they split up into two teams. Wakankar and Vaidya approached the boundary wall from the rear while the others crept up from the front. When they were close enough,

---

218 Sinari, p. 117.

they dropped down on their bellies and crawled to the rear entrance, from where they fired twice. There was no response from the building. They fired again. There was a loud thump this time, and then again, silence. Not knowing what to make of it, Wakankar ran to the door, kicked it open and shouted in Portuguese, 'Vem fora!' (come out). He was met with silence. The house seemed deserted. But scattered all around was proof of recent occupation—cigarette butts, empty liquor bottles, leftover food.

By this time, the others had entered through the front door and together, they searched the house thoroughly. In the kitchen, hidden under a cot, they found the owner of the place, the Brahmin of Rakholi. The plump, richly attired man crawled out and fell prostrate before them, begging them to spare his life. He had no option but to help the Portuguese, he told them. They had stayed in his house for a day and left the following afternoon.

After assuring him that he would be safe under the new administration, Wakankar and his men walked up to the river. It was flowing well over the causeway, so they knew they had no option but to wait. It was dark when they returned to Silvassa, determined to launch the final assault the day the waters receded. It would be a week before that became possible.[219]

On 7 August, Lawande held another press conference in Silvassa and announced that on 15 August, Independence Day would be celebrated all over Dadra and Nagar Haveli. This meant that Fidaldo and his forces would have to be subjugated before that date, which seemed a tall order. They were firmly entrenched, superior in numbers and better armed, while the Dal volunteers were only a handful and

---

219 Vaidya, p. 19–20.

had limited resources.[220] Moreover, the communist-backed Warlis had reached Surangi by now, after occupying parts of Nagar Haveli. As the road to Khanvel passed through Surangi, and the section of Warlis led by the Goan People's Party also wanted control of Khanvel, conflict seemed inevitable. The biggest and seemingly insurmountable obstacle, though, was the Daman Ganga, which was in a state of flood.[221]

It was the Brahmin of Rakholi who came to their help. He suggested they contact the Warli toddy trappers, who were used to crossing the river even in such conditions, using rafts made by tying together logs from wild date trees. Sinari accepted the advice enthusiastically, gave the trader some money and asked him to get a raft made for them.[222]

Back in Silvassa, Lawande called for an urgent meeting. Dali Mancherji Vaidya had arrived with the latest updates.

Dali was a prominent landowner from Surangi. He was not only one of the most respected residents of Nagar Haveli but also wielded considerable clout in business circles in Bombay. He was related to Nagarwala and enjoyed a close rapport with him, which meant he could move freely between Lavachha, Vapi and Nagar Haveli. Though known to be one of the fairest employers in Nagar Haveli, he was often targeted by the communists, who had once infamously held his father, Mancherji, captive and made him rub his nose at their feet. The day after Silvassa's liberation, Dali arrived in Silvassa seeking protection and justice.

---

220 Lawande, p. 223
221 Vaidya, p. 33.
222 Sinari, p. 118.

Lawande sent Pilaji Jadhav in his jeep to accompany Dali to his estate. On the borders of the estate, Jadhav noticed some activity by the roadside—a few people carrying rifles and machetes were crouched behind the bushes. When Dali indicated to him that these were the men he had been referring to, Pilaji fired his gun in the air. Realising that Dali had the protection of the new regime, the troublemakers bolted.

Dali visited Silvassa once more to thank them and gave them the latest news—George Waz, Ivan Menezes, Mario Rodriguez and other leaders of the Goan People's Party had, with the help of the Warlis, reached Surangi, vandalised the distillery at Khadoli and occupied the police station at Khanvel. When the Dal leaders asked if he could help them by finding out the enemy's latest position, he promised to do so.

The next day, he returned with both good and bad news. The good news was that the riverside skirmish with the Portuguese had demoralised the Warlis. Hearing that the Portuguese were marching in from Dapada, they had abandoned their post in Khanvel and returned to their villages. The communist leaders had also retreated, along with a handful of armed Warlis, to Velugaon, a hamlet deep in the jungles. Conflict with them was not an immediate threat.

The bad news was that the Portuguese were firmly entrenched in Khanvel and determined to fight it out. Dali detailed to them the topography of the Khanvel police station and explained that since it was sandbagged from all sides and built on a higher level, it would be extremely difficult to mount an attack on it.[223]

It had been seven days since the fall of Silvassa. What had worked in favour of the Dal so far was the low morale of

---

223 Vaidya, p. 34.

the Portuguese because of the false narrative they had fallen for: that they were dealing with special armed forces sent by the Indian government. Once the bubble burst, and the Portuguese realised that the invaders were amateurs with more bluster and zeal than weaponry and training, they might return and easily drive them away.[224]

Lawande convened a meeting the same afternoon to finalise their strategy. Sinari proposed that the volunteers cross over on the morning of 10 August and position themselves around the Khanvel police station by dusk. He believed that a direct assault could result in the loss of lives, but he was also certain they would be able to secure victory. The Pune group thought this idea to be suicidal. They argued this could only result in a deadly rout. A cordon, they suggested, was appropriate, by which they could also cut off access to food and drink. The cordon would force Fidaldo to surrender without the Dal exposing its hand. The Goa group, however, termed this cowardice. The meeting did not resolve their differences, so they decided to play it by the ear. Lawande announced that a vehicle would leave for Rakholi at 6 a.m. the following day and instructed all those who wished to be part of the attacking team to present themselves at the police headquarters at 5.30 a.m.[225]

The next morning, each team member was issued a Lee Enfield 303 rifle, several rounds of ammunition, a Star pistol and two extra magazines for it. The group of over twenty included thirteen volunteers from Goa under Sinari and

---

224 Ibid.
225 Ibid, p. 37.

Prabhakar Vaidya, seven from the RSS under Kajrekar and Wakankar, and two newcomers, Bacchubhai and Gajjubhai, who were Azad Gomantak Dal members from Daman. They were accompanied by a Warli guide.

The group arrived at Rakholi before 7 a.m. but found to their dismay that the raft was too small to accommodate everyone. The water had receded a bit but was still flowing above the causeway and its markers, so the raft was still the only way to cross the turbulent river. The riverbed was rocky near the causeway, so the team tied a thick rope to the raft and dragged it 600 meters upstream where the river was wider and the current a little less threatening. The first batch of seven got into the raft, and a Warli man joined them with a fifteen-foot pole. They had travelled almost halfway before the depth of the river exceeded the height of the pole and the raft went into free flow. At a quick command from Sinari, the men squatted down and used their arms to row to the other bank. Jumping into the water, they dragged the raft ashore, then sent it back. The three trips required to transport everyone took two hours, and it was 9 a.m. by the time the last person crossed over.[226]

As they sent the raft back one last time, they knew their last link with Silvassa had been severed.

Taking the main road to Dapada would have been risky, so Sinari asked their guide to take them through the jungle paths to meet the main road a few hundred metres from Dapada. Conscious that they were in enemy territory, they stopped to load their rifles. The rain had mercifully ceased by this time, and the only sounds they could hear were the wet plodding of their boots and the occasional croak of a bullfrog.

---

226 Ibid, p. 39.

The guide led the way, Sinari fifty feet behind him. The others followed in single file in small groups six feet apart. The guide carried both a red flag and a white one. Sinari had instructed him to hold the white one up while walking and raise the red flag in case of danger.

It took them ninety minutes to get to Dapada. As the road came into view, they stopped and approached the town from two different directions. Sinari and five others parted ways to encircle the village and approach it from the north while the other group, with Kajrekar in the lead, entered from the south. They walked in teams of three, each giving the other cover from behind. As he inched forward carefully, Kanhoba Naik suddenly gestured to the rest to stop, then fired in the air. They saw someone trying to run away into the undergrowth, and collapse. There was a shout of 'Mari gayo!' (I've been killed). The person's response to Naik's warning shot was so extreme, Kajrekar and his team assumed there was a hidden threat, possibly the Portuguese lying in wait to ambush them. They lay down and cocked their rifles, but nothing happened. It soon became clear that there were no Portuguese in the vicinity. Inching closer to the person still lying face down in the muck, they found him scared but alive. It was one of the Warlis who had run away into the jungles when the Portuguese approached. Assuming it was safer now, he had come back to check on his possessions. They lifted him up and assured him they were not the enemy.

The man, now a lot calmer, told them that the tribals of Surangi, led by the Goan People's Party, had vandalised the distillery. Also, the Portuguese had beaten up the residents of villages near Dapada and made away with their grain, chicken and goats. He confirmed that the communist-led group had run away from Khanvel when the Portuguese appeared. As far as he knew, there were no Portuguese in Dapada.

Moving slowly, the group reached Dapada and arrived at the police post, which was the pre-decided meeting point. Sinari and his team joined them there. They made tea, ate some of the biscuits and bread they had carried from Silvassa and moved on to Khanvel, refreshed.[227]

Their next stop was the Keni distillery. Just outside the distillery walls was a well from which they drew water for drinking. As they refilled their bottles and sat down to rest under a tree, there was a series of alarming sounds—a deep, low snort, followed by a mighty bellow and the sound of heavy hooves hitting wet earth. The men turned and found an angry, drunk buffalo charging straight at them.

The buffalo belonged to one of the guards and was usually tied up near the quarters, but during the attack by the Warlis, she had broken loose and, through a breach in the compound wall, wandered into the distillery. There, she had drunk to her heart's content the liquor that had spilt out of the numerous cans that the Warlis had thrown around. When she saw these strange men drinking from the well that was rightfully hers, she charged.

Her aggressive dash drove some of the volunteers up the distillery wall and others up the tree under which she stood snorting and stamping, daring them to come down. It was only when one of them fired a few shots from the pistol at her hooves that she probably realised that being a property owner came with some troublesome stipulations, and fled into the jungle.[228] Shaken but amused, the volunteers drank their fill of the well water and continued on the road to Khanvel.[229]

---

227 Lawande, pp. 228–229.

228 Sinari, p. 119.

229 In conversation with Sanjay Raut.

Showdown

AT first sight, the Khanvel site appeared impregnable. The patelado was located at a crossroads, where the roads from Dapada, Kherwa, Udhawa and Khanvel met. It was at least twenty feet above the road, giving the Portuguese the higher ground. The police station stood behind it, parallel to the road from Khanvel. Sandbags encircled both the police station and the patelado, and from the open windows of both, the muzzles of rifles jutted out, gleamed wickedly in the sun. Behind the two buildings was another, smaller building, which their guide told them was the storeroom and cookhouse. To the south, on the opposite side of the road, lay the imposing Pilar Mission Church, of which only the spire was visible. Between the volunteers and the church lay fields of millet, and further at the back, the jungle stretched as far as the eye could see. On the Kherva road, 200 metres or so from the police station, was a dilapidated single-storey building that looked like an outhouse. The guide told them this was the forest guard house and it was probably empty because all the guards would have been sent off to join the defending force.[230]

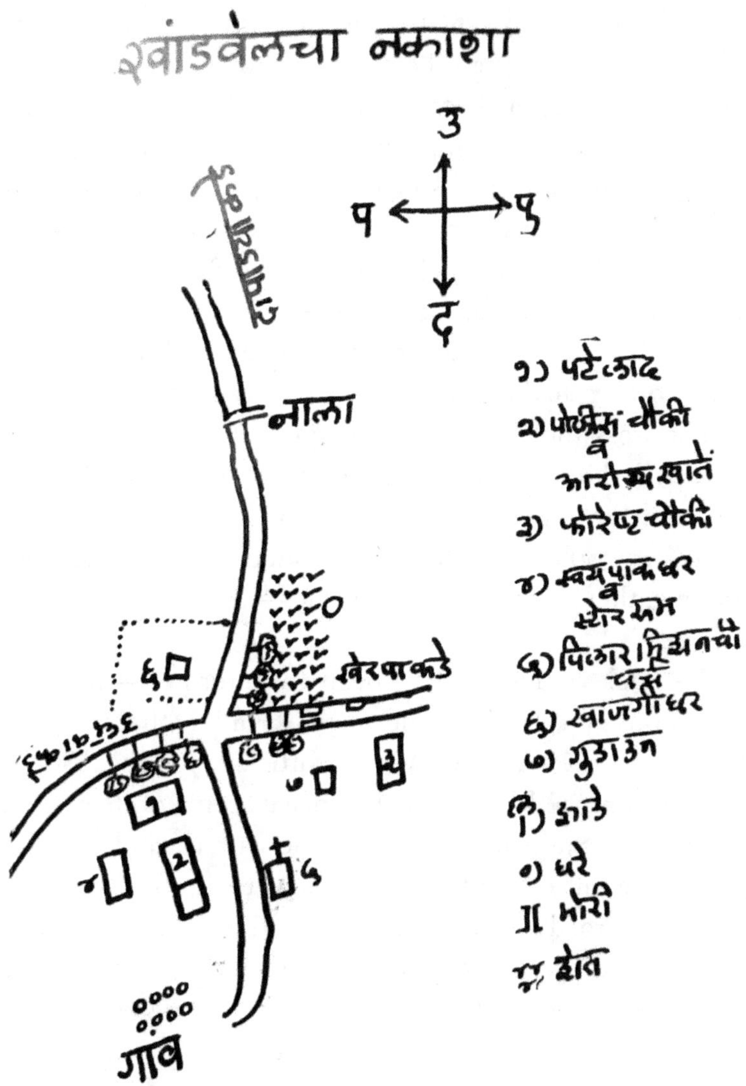

Rough map of the police post and surrounding buildings in Khanvel drawn up by Prabhakar Vaidya based on his own observations

---

230 Vaidya, p. 49.

The volunteers split into three teams with the intention of pinning the Portuguese to the police station and choking off their supplies. The first group, led by Sinari, moved westwards. They planned to cross the Udhawa road and take up positions behind the cookhouse. The second, with Prabhakar Vaidya, stayed where it was because they intended to take a stand behind a small building between their position and the patelado. Reaching the small building meant crossing the Dapada road from where the Portuguese expected an attack and on which they had trained their guns. Still, given the tree cover, they felt this was manageable.

The third team, consisting of Thalee and Kanhoba Naik among others, had the most straightforward task—they were to first cross the fields, then the Kherva road, and take up position behind the trees that grew between the Khanvel road and the forest guard house. Confident that the dense tree cover would allow them to remain unseen from the main building, they walked into the bushes—to be met with a hail of bullets.

The Dal volunteers had been misinformed—the forest guard house was far from unoccupied. Finding that the police station and the patelado were insufficient for the 150-odd men he commanded, Fidaldo had placed some of them in the guard house. Surrounded by trees, and with the police station and square out of sight, they had kept their guns trained on the Dapada road and the fields. They had spotted Naik's group as soon as they started moving through the fields towards them. Mercifully for the volunteers, the Portuguese jumped the gun, so to speak, and began firing before the enemy was in range. The volunteers dived into the fields and disappeared from view. They were safe, but trapped.

Hearing the shots, the group led by Prabakhar Vaidya raced to take up position behind the house opposite the patelado. In order to get in, they had to first break through the surrounding fence. The noise alerted the policemen in the patelado, who started shooting at them. Vaidya's team crept through a gap in the tree cover and, crawling through the rear courtyard, settled down in a small ditch. The Portuguese in the patelado could not see them but kept firing in their direction, the bullets whizzing harmlessly over their heads. The volunteers returned fire, but the shots bounced off the iron grills of the window, perhaps because the building was situated at a height. Vaidya and Dattaram Desai then raced to the other side of the road, ducking under the hail of gunfire.

While both sides continued to fire, neither had much luck. One stray bullet fired by the volunteers must have hit someone inside because a shout of 'Mari gayo!' was heard.[231] The shutters were immediately swung to a near close, and the firing continuing from between the gaps.[232]

Prabhakar Vaidya noted that the Portuguese had not fired in the direction of Sinari's group. He realised that the Portuguese had probably not noticed them, and to retain an ace in the hole, kept the Portuguese distracted with intermittent firing from his end. The Sinari team lay low, waiting to spring their advantage.[233]

It was growing dark. The Portuguese did not know the strength of the attackers and were uncertain about their strategy. The Dal volunteers knew they were grossly outnumbered and that the terrain was against them— entering the buildings by force was out of the question. It was a classic stalemate. Kajrekar knew he desperately needed

---

231 Vaidya, pp. 50–52.
232 Lawande, p. 232–234.
233 Ibid.

a force multiplier, so he withdrew and headed to Surangi to talk to Jatruben Vansabhai Ghoom.

—

The forest-dwellers near Khanvel belonged to one of two tribes—Warli or Kokna. Whereas the Warlis were impoverished and eked out a living by working on the lands of the big landlords or tilling their own small patches and rearing chickens and goats, the Koknas were landowners with considerable influence. And no one was more influential than Jatruben Vansabhai Ghoom.[234]

Ghoom commanded respect across the belt of thirty-three villages around Khanvel, not so much for the amount of land she possessed but for the force of her personality. Tall and stately in her thirties, she was probably the only tribal woman in the area who owned and rode a horse. For any tribal who got into trouble with the administration, her house was the first port of call, and she never disappointed them. The legend was that once, when she entered the Khanvel police station and the officer in charge did not get up to receive her, she kicked the chair away from under him.[235] Such was her aura that the police took no action against her. Instead, the officer apologised and saluted her.

The Portuguese, however, got their revenge by involving her husband Vansabhai in a false murder case and sentencing him to life in prison. He was sent to the infamous Diu jail located on an island off the Diu coast, from where, it was said, no one returned alive. Enraged by this, she took upon herself the task of motivating the tribals, going from village to village

---

234 In conversation with Deepak Jadhav.
235 In conversation with Sanjay Raut.

and delivering fiery speeches urging them to overthrow the Portuguese. It was most likely her mobilisation that resulted in the tribals getting together under the communists. However, the firefight with the Portuguese across the river a few days earlier had not only scared the tribals and driven them back into their villages, it had also sent the leaders of the Goan People's Party into hiding in Velugaon.[236]

It was to Ghoom that Kajrekar headed with his request for reinforcements.

As per the prevalent system, the Portuguese collected half the produce of any household in the area as tax. Whether it was their crop, the eggs their hens laid or the milk from their goats, half went to the tax collectors or to the police station. In addition, the station sent a policeman every morning to one of the surrounding villages. If he placed a wooden staff outside any house, chosen at random, the household would have to not only deliver the day's rations to the police station but also serve the station staff by cooking, cleaning, etc. This was over and above the tax they had to pay.

On the morning of 10 August, the day after the Portuguese column marched into Khanvel, they ordered a forest guard to fetch them a cow, as was their wont. He chanced upon a pregnant cow and, placing the wooden staff in front of the house nearby, untied the cow and took her away. The cow was slaughtered in full public view, cooked and eaten.

Tempers ran high throughout the day. The slaughter of a pregnant cow was unacceptable to most people. Into this tinder box stepped Kajrekar with his plea for help. Ghoom

---

236 In conversation with Rasmi Bheema Dhangda.

immediately mounted her horse and offered another to Kajrekar. All night, they went from village to village, addressing the locals. Their message was simple: 'We must fight! There is no need to fear the Portuguese. They are now confined to Khanvel. Let us stand against them together and throw them out.' Ghoom demanded they use whatever weapons they had and join the attack—it was their last opportunity. If they missed it, the Portuguese would never stop mistreating them.

Tribals from villages like Garh Chichala, Deshi Dabhadi, Kherdi, Surangi, as well as padas around Khanvel responded with enthusiasm. Local leaders like Rama Karbhari from Kherdi, Vajya Kankad from Surangi, Cheta Kadoo from Velugaon and Jetra Bhenda Misaal from Khanvel passed on the message to every hut and hovel. Tribals came out of their houses carrying locally fabricated pellet guns, licensed rifles, swords, spears, bows and arrows and gathered near the Khanvel police station. As the numbers increased, more and more people found the courage to step out of their homes. Soon, there were enough of them to surround the police station from all sides. At daybreak on 11 August, the firing began again.

~

The forest guards were the first to be neutralised. Creeping up to the building, Desai and his team discovered a small alcove behind it, probably used for bathing, with a waist-level boundary wall around it. From here, they could fire directly into the guard house. Before Desai's team discovered this vantage point, they had nowhere to take a stand, and had been shot at with impunity. Now, for the first time, the Portuguese were under fire. They scrambled for shelter and shut all the doors and windows, firing only from between gaps of the window shutters, which limited their range of attack and motion.[237]

While the Desai team faced the firing from the forest guard house, the other two volunteer units, aided by the tribals, opened fire at the police station and the patelado. The Portuguese returned fire, but there was a difference this time. The tribals knew every tree and hillock in the area, and they clambered up and found vantage points for themselves, taking their new allies with them. There was an old peepal tree just opposite the police station, which had a huge trunk and branches that towered over the station's entrance. The heavy foliage offered the men a hiding place, and the height gave them the advantage of shooting downward at their enemy. Finally, their bullets could penetrate the station.

Some of the attackers entered the church, went up to its roof and bell tower and fired into the patelado. Now, the roles were reversed. The bullets shot by the Portuguese fell well short and Fidaldo's forces were exposed to all sorts of projectiles from above. His men were outnumbered, under siege, and beginning to sustain injuries. For the first time since entering Khanvel, Fidaldo was in distress.

The battle could have continued indefinitely, or at least till the ammunition on either side ran out. However, that would have meant a lengthy standoff and each side had its own concerns about that. The Portuguese feared that if they ran out of ammunition and stopped firing their guns, the tribals would storm the police station and, with their newfound aggression, probably hack each one of them to pieces. The Dal feared the possibility, unlikely as it was, of reinforcements suddenly arriving from Daman, or being forced to withdraw

---

237 Vaidya, p. 52.

due to orders from Morarji Desai. Morarji Desai himself was apprehensive of central intervention and keen on a quick resolution lest the decision to permit the Dal to enter Nagar Haveli cost him politically.

Everyone wanted a quick solution to the standoff. It was time then for some backchannel diplomacy.

The man chosen for this was Bhagubhai Bhandari.[238]

Bhagubhai Bhandari was usually wary of the police. After all, his livelihood depended on smuggling liquor from Nagar Haveli into Gujarat, where it was prohibited. It was rumoured that he did not stop at liquor smuggling but also brought gold from the Middle East into Nagar Haveli and sold it inside Gujarat. At the lower levels of the administration, though, he had extensive contacts both on the Portuguese and the Indian side. He had also made inroads into the tribal population, since he used some of them as couriers and their homes as temporary safe houses for his illicit wares. His reputation was that of someone willing to take risks if offered enough money.

When Nagarwala, on Morarji's instructions, started looking for someone to act as a mediator, Bhandari's name came up often. Why he agreed to mediate between the two warring factions, whether it was for money or to placate the law, is unknown. Whatever the reason, he walked alone into the war zone on the evening of 11 August, a white flag in his hand, and negotiated a ceasefire.

The initiative for the ceasefire had come from the governor of Daman, who had had a decided change of heart about ordering his men to stand up against the rebels at all

---

238 In conversation with Deepak Jadhav.

costs now that they had been cornered in Khanvel by the furious tribals.. Earlier, when the United Goans liberated Dadra on 24 July, he had attempted to cross the border with an armed militia, but the Special Reserve Police had denied him access. When Silvassa fell, he sought permission once again from the Indian government to send soldiers from Daman through Indian territory, but was refused. Now, with the Portuguese forces under siege in Khanvel, the governor persisted in his attempts to send reinforcements, but the Indian side denied permission yet again.

Left with no option but to minimise the damage, he decided on backchannel diplomacy to effect a surrender of Fidaldo's garrison. He could not have communicated directly with the Indian government as it would have compromised the Portuguese claim to Dadra and Nagar Haveli, so he established contact through the Spanish Embassy in Delhi. His only request was that Fidaldo and his forces be allowed to leave Dadra and Nagar Haveli safely. Accepting the request suited the Indian side since a massacre of the Portuguese forces would have caused an international incident.

Instructions went down from Delhi to Bombay to Lavachha to find someone to negotiate an unofficial surrender, and they found Bhandari.

Bhandari conveyed the hopelessness of the situation to Fidaldo and the near-zero possibility of getting reinforcements. He informed Fidaldo that if he and his forces marched the nine kilometres to Udhawa, Nagarwala would personally take them into custody and arrange for them to travel to Bombay and thence to Goa.

His pitch to the tribals and the Azad Gomantak Dal was that the Portuguese were entrenched and had adequate ammunition to continue the battle for a long time. If they permitted the surrender and gave safe passage to them,

Khanvel and the whole of Nagar Haveli would become free at once.

Both sides agreed to the terms, and a temporary ceasefire was announced. Fidaldo and his forces left the Khanvel police station and surrendered to Nagarwala on 11 August. By the next morning, the fighting should have stopped, but at the start of the day, the sound of gunfire was heard once more from inside the patelado.[239]

—

After the surrender, most of the tribals had returned to their villages. The volunteers were left with little support and rushed to take up their old positions when they heard the gunfire. Naik and his team had not relaxed their vigil since the men inside the guard house were still firing sporadically. Prabhakar Vaidya and his squad, assisted by a few tribals, took up positions behind the same small building they had occupied previously and began firing at the patelado. Sinari and his team crept to the cookhouse and came under a hail of bullets. Diving into the shrubbery, Sinari noticed a Portuguese officer running in a crouch from the patelado to the police station, wielding a Sten gun. As the man turned to enter the police station, Sinari, disregarding personal safety, rose, sprinted and lunged at him. Before he could recover, Sinari snatched his weapon and placed a pistol to his head. Begging for his life, the man identified himself as Sub-inspector Perreira. Sinari threatened to shoot him instantly if he did not order everyone inside to surrender. Believing they were grossly outnumbered, thirty-one policemen came out of

---

239 In conversation with Deepak Jadhav.

the police station one by one and capitulated. Some of them were so drunk they could hardly handle their weapons, which Sinari's team swiftly confiscated.[240]

Prabhakar Vaidya then raised his voice and ordered those inside the patelado to surrender. Seeing their officer and the other policemen standing with their hands raised, the twenty men inside the patelado also yielded. The volunteers herded them all into the open area outside the police station. Sinari directed them to get down on the ground with their hands behind their backs. Volunteers were posted a few feet apart to guard them. After giving orders to shoot if anyone so much as moved, Sinari marched Perreira to the forest guard house. Seeing their officer approach with his hands raised, the men inside realised the game was up and surrendered.

Perriera confirmed that Fidaldo, Falcao, Pedado and a hundred other men had marched to Udhawa the previous night. Although Fidaldo's intention was to surrender, he had ordered Perreira to tell the others that he was leaving to get reinforcements from Daman. Perreira was to provide covering fire if required and join them at Udhawa as soon as possible. There were no instructions for the others left behind—presumably, they were to be abandoned to their fate.

They took a headcount and found that except for those that had marched out under Fidaldo, almost everyone was accounted for. Sinari directed the volunteers to search all the buildings. In the patelado and the police station building, they found only ammunition and empty liquor bottles. In the health centre next to the police station, Prabhakar Vaidya saw a door open and heard the sound of someone running away. As he gave chase, the person darted into the cookhouse, then

---

240 Sinari, p. 123.

turned and fired at him with his revolver. Luckily for Vaidya, there was only the sound of a click—the pistol had jammed. Vaidya barrelled into the man and snatched his weapon. The last of the policemen had been arrested. Khanvel and the entire region of Dadra and Nagar Haveli were now free of Portuguese dominion.[241]

Soon afterwards, some of the volunteers noticed some activity in the church and found the parish priest and two other church officials hiding in a room at the rear. They also found two other middle-aged men taking cover in the church. The men identified themselves as R. Menezes and Dr Allero, the Patel and medical officer, respectively. They had been in hiding since the time the volunteers surrounded the police station and had been without food or water for almost two days, fearing for their lives. Having been fed the propaganda that the volunteers were uncivilised and cruel, these men, who had expected to meet a brutal end, were surprised when Sinari offered them water and assured them that the church would not be vandalised. He also requested Allero to treat the injured and asked Menezes if he would help them with the administration.

It was around 2 p.m., and everyone was hungry. The parish priest stepped up to arrange a simple but tasty meal of dal and rice, and everyone, including the Portuguese prisoners, ate with relish. Naik went to the local trader's shop and asked for something sweet to celebrate their victory. Since

---

241 Lawande, pp. 238–239.

nothing was available, he returned with some sugar[242] which he distributed to everyone to mark the occasion.[243]

Sinari drafted a detailed report on the operation for Lawande, who was stationed in Silvassa. He asked for a bus to transport the prisoners to Silvassa since there weren't enough resources in Khanvel to guard and feed so many. A local landlord loaned them a horse and one of the volunteers, Dattaram, accompanied by Lahanu, their Warli guide, left with the letter at about 4 p.m.

By about 4.45 p.m., Warlis from the neighbouring areas began to troop into the compound of the Khanvel police post. Sinari raised the tricolour and addressed the 300-odd people gathered there. He appealed to all those who had fled their villages to return to them.

'With the surrender of the Portuguese policemen today, the Azad Gomantak Dal has overthrown the evil Portuguese regime. All of us will celebrate 15 August as the Independence Day of Dadra and Nagar Haveli,' he said. 'On that day, speaking in Silvassa, the president of the Dal, Vishvanath Lawande, will ask the Indian government to merge Dadra and Nagar Haveli with the Indian Union. While the government considers this appeal, the Azad Gomantak Dal will administer the liberated territories. We want to hand over these territories at the earliest, either to the Indian government or to all of you.'

---

242 In Maharashtra, the distribution of sweets to celebrate a happy occasion is colloquially referred to as 'sakhar watane' which means the distribution of sugar. This came true in literal terms in Khanvel that day.

243 Vaidya, p. 59.

After dividing sentry duty among themselves, the volunteers retired to bed, unaware that yet another roadblock awaited them the following day.[244]

~

The next morning, by the time everyone had freshened up and had a round of chai and biscuits, a letter arrived to further lift their spirits. In it, Lawande confirmed that Fidaldo and his associates had surrendered to Nagarwala in Udhawa and had been sent to Bombay under armed escort.

A group of volunteers headed by Bacchubhai and Gajjubhai were detailed to escort the remaining prisoners in Khanvel to Rakholi, where a bus awaited them on the other side of the river to take them to Silvassa. Fortunately, the river water had receded and the causeway was visible, so crossing it was far easier this time. Also, the prisoners were clearly told that anyone who attempted to escape would be shot.

Sinari and Kajrekar then went from village to village on horseback to update the locals on the situation. They also recruited three Warlis from the nearby hamlets, offering them a salary of ₹3 a day (a princely sum then). They gave them a day's wage as advance and asked them to gather information about the activities of any pro-Portuguese elements in their areas.

With the prisoners sent away and a final confirmation about the surrender of the Portuguese received, things were looking up. Dr Alluro had taken charge of the health centre and made it functional. Sinari had requested Menezes to wait till 15 August before taking control of the patelado. For

____

244 Lawande, p. 240.

the first time since the start of the campaign, they were all beginning to relax a little.

That's when a jeep drove into Khanvel and an injured and bleeding Kajrekar stepped out of it.

Kajrekar told them that after accompanying the prisoners to Rakholi, he had started on the return journey when he ran into some trouble in the jungles near Dapada. Apparently, a group of heavily armed men of the Goan People's Party under Captain Gole and George Vaz, aided by forty-odd tribals, had gathered near Dapada. They had shouted slogans and opened fire at him. Luckily, only one bullet grazed him, leaving a deep furrow on his cheek.

Although this was alarming, the volunteers decided against retaliation. After Kajrekar was administered first aid, Sinari ordered that the arms seized from the arrested policemen and forest guards be loaded into a jeep for transportation to Silvassa. Since it was dangerous cargo and the area seemed hostile, he sent Thalee, Naik and Tukaram in another vehicle along with Kajrekar. Their instructions were to fire a warning shot into the air if the communist-led Warlis tried to stop them, but to shoot to kill if they continued to feel threatened. Under no circumstances were they to let their weapons fall into the wrong hands.

Thankfully, they did not encounter anyone on the way. The weapon-laden jeep driven by Kajrekar crossed the now calm river at a shallow point and headed to Silvassa. But on the way back, the others saw a lot of activity in the Warli settlement just outside Dapada. They were told that Vaz, Gole and a few others had gathered in the jungles. They were planning to attack some landlords in Surangi, loot cash and weapons and march onward to Khanvel.

The volunteers rushed back to Khanvel at breakneck speed. Kajrekar told Sinari what they had heard, but he refused to initiate any action based on hearsay. But when Lahanu overheard the mention of lal baotas, he told them that he had observed the communist group near his village and their leaders had been enquiring about the strength of the Dal volunteers in Khanvel. Still unwilling to initiate action against his fellow Goans without proof, Sinari summoned the Warlis they had employed to validate the facts.

Very early on the morning of 14 August, Lahanu confirmed that the lal baotas and a few Warlis were planning to attack a landlord in Surangi and march onwards to Khanvel after seizing supplies from him. Two others arrived a little after Lahanu and verified this information. Both Sinari and Kajrekar were in agreement now that it was imperative to act.

The volunteers split into two groups. The first, under Thalee, stayed back to guard Khanvel while the other, led by Sinari and Vaidya, set off for Surangi. Sinari was still hesitant to cross swords with other Goans and felt that patrolling the area might be enough of a deterrent. They had just set off when Lahanu, who had gone ahead to scope out the situation, came running back, looking anxious. He told them that a group of armed Warlis, around forty in number, led by Vaz and a few others, were marching towards Khanvel. They would reach in the next thirty minutes.[245]

---

245 Vaidya, p. 71.

The situation was grave. If an armed mob led by the Goan People's Party was approaching Khanvel despite knowing it was under the control of the Azad Gomantak Dal, it meant their intentions were not honourable. Sinari and Vaidya agreed that it was best not to be caught in the main square in case of a confrontation. They decided to head the intruders off at the border and sent a message to the police station asking the others to catch up with them on the Dapada road as soon as possible. Then they rushed towards the edge of the village, and not a moment too soon. The mob led by George Vaz was barely a hundred yards away and marching determinedly towards them.

Sinari directed all the others to occupy a dry nullah nearby, and they scampered into place while he and Vaidya stood in the middle of the road, directly in the line of fire.

It was tense. In his deep, sonorous voice, Sinari commanded the intruders to halt. Mercifully, barely a few yards from them, Vaz brought the group to a standstill. Most of the Goans in the mob, including Vaz, were known to Sinari. He addressed Vaz, demanding to know why they were marching towards Khanvel. 'Turn back,' said Sinari, 'and go home. The fight is over.'

Vaz refused. Khanvel, he claimed, belonged to the Goan People's Party since they had captured it first. If the Dal wanted to stop them, they would have to mow them down with bullets. The threat, delivered quite casually, shook Sinari. He did not want to shoot at people who were once allies. Seeing Sinari falter, Prabhakar Vaidya stepped into the altercation.[246]

'You did not capture Khanvel,' he told Vaz bluntly. 'You occupied it because the police station had already

---

246 In conversation with Shefali Vaidya.

been vacated. That is not an act of liberation but of mere occupation. Even if you consider it liberation, why did you run away when Fidaldo and Falcao got here? And even if you did run, why did you not return to take it back?'

Vaz was disinterested in logic. He said he was not going to argue with them but was determined to enter Khanvel, at least for a while.

Seeing that he could not be moved, Vaidya agreed to escort the group into Khanvel, provided they left their weapons behind. He added that the offer did not extend to the Warlis accompanying them. Most of them had criminal records and would be arrested if they entered Khanvel. He gave Vaz ten minutes to decide. Any delay, he said, would leave him with no alternative but to fire at the mob.

Boldly, Vaidya turned his back to them and ordered the Dal volunteers to load their weapons. Vaz had hitherto thought that the Dal would not fire at them, but upon seeing the guns being loaded, he went into a huddle with some of the other men, including the Warlis. An argument seemed to erupt, with some gesticulating in the direction of Dapada, perhaps suggesting a retreat, while others appeared determined to move forward. To hasten the decision-making, Vaidya bade the volunteers to fire over the heads of the Goans. As the bullets whizzed past them, all quarrels ceased. Realising that Vaidya was serious, Vaz signalled to him to halt and demanded to know if they were prepared to accept his condition, which was that Vaz, with a few colleagues, would enter Khanvel, stay there for a while and then leave. He said he wanted to send a colleague, Keshav Talwalikar, to the base near Udhawa to update Godavaribai Parulekar and other members of the party, so they would know what had been decided. Vaidya accepted this and gestured at Naik and Tukaram to follow

Keshav. He also had the Goans and the Warlis deposit their weapons, which the Dal volunteers took into their custody.

As the Goans, under the armed escort of the volunteers, trooped into the main square of Khanvel, some of the Warlis who had previously been aligned with them but had fought alongside the Dal, started trickling in to meet them. All seemed peaceful, until two hours later, when Tukaram and Naik walked in holding a gun to Keshav's head. They upturned the cloth bag he had been carrying and showed everyone what he had been trying to smuggle back from Parulekar's camp—three pistols and ammunition. The Goans had every intention of creating trouble, hoping that the Warlis who had been their associates would now help them throw out the Dal.

Knowing that they had been exposed, Vaz and some of the other party members started hollering slogans in the main square, trying to sow chaos. Seeing through their act, Vaidya and his team surrounded, arrested and locked them up in the patelado. The very next day, they were transferred under armed guard to Silvassa. Sinari personally accompanied them, along with Bhopale and a few others.

On 14 August, leaving behind ten volunteers to protect Khanvel, Vaidya and the rest of the team left for Silvassa, where preparations were underway to celebrate the Indian Independence Day and the liberation of Dadra and Nagar Haveli from Portuguese rule.

14 August 1954

Unification

WHILE the battle for Khanvel raged, Lawande, who had stayed back in Silvassa, set into motion the process of streamlining the administration of the territories. When the captive police officers from Khanvel arrived in Silvassa, Wakankar separated the locals who had worked for the previous regime from those who had surrendered in Khanvel and locked them up in separate rooms. He noted their names and designations and made each one sign a document of surrender. In consultation with Nagarwala, it was decided that those among them who expressed interest in working with the new administration could stay back, while the rest would be escorted via Vapi to Portuguese-controlled Daman.[247]

The officers who chose to stay back were assured of the same pay and privileges they had been accustomed to. Lawande promised them a raise if they worked with integrity but told them in no uncertain terms that they would be

---

247 Lawande, p. 245.

dealt with firmly if they continued to bother and exploit the citizens. Karpurkar, the secretary of the treasury, and Bhonsle, the secretary to the previous administrator, as well as a few others agreed to work with the new dispensation and swore to be loyal.

All the arms and ammunition recovered were listed and deposited in the armoury. Varnekar from the Dal and Zanzale from Pune were made responsible for guarding the arsenal and instructed not to issue a single weapon to anyone unless authorised in writing by the administration. Lawande requested Karpurkar to continue handling the treasury, subject to his control and direction. Karmalkar, an experienced administrator, teamed up with Lawande to review the work of the various departments. Department heads were to continue as before and report to Karmalkar and Kajrekar. [248]

On 12 August, Morarji Desai deputed Lalbhai Naik, a leader of the Gujarat Pradesh Congress Committee and his confidant to visit Silvassa and assess the situation. Naik spoke with Lawande and his team and interacted closely with the local population, community leaders and government officials. In his report to the chief minister, he expressed his satisfaction with the new administration.

The Congress Seva Dal[249] volunteers accompanying Naik played a crucial role in consolidating the gains of the struggle. They split into groups of four and travelled to the villages

---

248 Lawande, p. 247.

249 The Congress Sewa Dal was set up in 1924 and was then called the Hindusthan Sewa Dal. Nehru was its first president. It was intended to be a cadre-based organisation whose members always wore a khadi topi and a white uniform. It was created to raise a force of disciplined workers to further the interests of the Congress party. The name was changed to Congress Sewa Dal in 1931.

in the liberated territories, even the most remote of them. Spending time in each town and village, they convinced the locals that the 'fanaga' were indeed gone and that the new administration would work for the benefit of the people. They carried the Indian flag with them and hoisted one in each place they visited. They worked for about a month and covered even the smallest communities, building bridges between the government and the local populace.

Naik also deputed two prominent locals, Dr Harisinh Paramar and Umedsinh Paramar, to talk to the local Christian families. Accompanied by G. Gregorio Coutinho, a leading light of the Christian community in Silvassa, they went from door to door and assured the families of their safety and security. About a hundred people expressed their desire to move to Daman, whereupon a truck was arranged to transport them to the border. In Daman, they joined their relatives living in the Portuguese territory.

In his capacity as the administrator, Lawande convened a meeting to which he invited the leaders of the Pune and Goa groups as well as prominent locals. It was resolved at the meeting that Lawande and Lad would go to Bombay the next day to thank Morarji Desai for his help and express their desire to continue the collaboration with his government to free first Daman, then Diu and Goa. As a token of appreciation, they would present him with a three-foot-long bejewelled, ivory-handled sword they had seized from the residence of Fidaldo.[250]

The attitude of the Azad Gomantak Dal volunteers towards the left-leaning Goan People's Party volunteers led by George Vaz differed from that of the RSS group. Whereas the former viewed them merely as allies with a different ideology, the

---

250 Lawande, p. 249.

RSS-led group viewed them as antagonists bent upon granting the benefits of liberation to one section of the locals at the cost of the others. The attack on some of the landlords by the communists and their attempts to rob them, as in the case of Dali Mancherji Vaidya, reinforced their prejudice. They felt that given the opportunity, the lal baotas would unleash a class war between the erstwhile 'haves' and the tribal 'have nots', resulting in chaos to the detriment of the liberated territories.

These conflicting views resulted in arguments between the two sides. While transporting the arrested Goan People's Party members to Silvassa, one such discussion had led to blows. Enraged by something one of the communists said, Bhopale had attacked him with his axe. Fortunately, the victim managed to dodge it and the axe hit a tree; otherwise, the blow was so powerful it would have split open his skull. Sinari had immediately disarmed Bhopale to discourage further conflict and restored a shaky peace.

Lawande met Vaz and his colleagues, along with Lad and Karmalkar, as soon as they reached Silvassa and attempted to figure out a solution. The Goan Peoples' Party leaders were adamant that they would not leave Dadra and Nagar Haveli. They reiterated their claim on the liberated territories, insisting that they had freed sixty-three of the seventy-two villages. The stalemate persisted, and they were locked up again for the night.

The matter was finally resolved on 15 August when the chief guest for the day's celebrations, Tristao de Braganza Cunha,[251] a veteran freedom fighter from Goa, arrived in Silvassa. With the sheer force of his personality, he managed

---

251 Cunha was known as the father of the Goan liberation movement. He was the founder of the Goa Congress Committee and had a legendary status amongst Goan freedom fighters.

to persuade the Goan People's Party to withdraw from Dadra and Nagar Haveli. Before leaving, Vaz gave a written undertaking that his party would never again interfere in the working of the liberated territories.[252]

The Dal wanted the day's celebrations to be a grand affair befitting the occasion. With the help of the locals and the administrative staff, the volunteers decorated the government buildings, and the tricolour proudly fluttered from every one of them. A vast procession set off from the main square at 8.30 a.m., led by a young man on horseback holding the tricolour aloft. Students, tribals, townsfolk and others marched in four columns. Winding through the streets of Silvassa, they reached the place where the flag was to be hoisted. Lawande, Sinari, Wakankar, Kajrekar and other leaders standing atop a stage decorated with garlands welcomed the procession. A hush descended on the gathering as chief guest Tristao de Braganza Cunha unfurled the Indian flag amidst the blowing of bugles. A shower of rose petals descended on the onlookers, and the crowd burst into wild applause as the Dal volunteers fired a twenty-one-gun salute. After a full-throated rendition of the Indian national anthem, the chief guest delivered his speech in English, which was translated into Gujarati and Marathi by one of the locals. The tribals, who did not understand what was being said until it was translated, still clapped enthusiastically whenever the townsfolk did. De Cunha then asked all the employees of the new regime to step forward and swear an oath pledging to serve the people of Dadra and Nagar Haveli with sincerity and devotion. A cheer went up

---

252 Lawande, p. 250.

as each person came up to the stage and committed to the service of the people.[253]

The next person to address the gathering was the administrator. Lawande spoke in Hindi, assuring the locals that the current arrangement was temporary, only meant to be in place until the formal union of the territories with India. He declared that the Azad Gomantak Dal would hand over power to elected representatives from amongst them, at the earliest. He also announced a slew of reforms that would be implemented in the next few days, including the abolishment of slavery and a tax cut on all produce from half to one-sixth, in addition to debt relief for the tribals. At this point, the crowd burst into its loudest round of frenzied cheering yet. Lawande added that all land would henceforth belong to the person tilling it and that a minimum wage would be declared and enforced. His speech included a warning—if any Portuguese loyalists resisted these reforms or attempted to sabotage them, they would have to answer to the administration.

Reiterating the goals of a Portuguese-free India, he stated that the Dal volunteers would retreat, resume training and begin planning the campaigns in Daman, Diu and Goa. He told the crowd that he had already petitioned the Maharashtra state government to urge the Centre to bring the liberated territories into the Indian Union as soon as possible.[254]

The retreat would happen much earlier than he expected, while the unification would take a full seven years.

---

253 Jyoti Deshpande, *Smritikalash*, Atharva Prakashan, Kolhapur, 2014, pp. 39–40.
254 Lawande, p. 253.

On 24 July, when the United Goans liberated Dadra, Paulo Bénard Guedes, the Governor-General of Portuguese India, sent an urgent message to the Government of India. In it, he mentioned the 'occupation of Dadra' by some unruly elements and expressed the fear that these groups may also attempt to attack Nagar Haveli. Guedes sought urgent permission from the Indian government to send soldiers through Indian territory to shore up the defences of Nagar Haveli. It was rumoured that he had deployed 1,000 Brazilian mercenaries to Daman and ordered them to massacre any intruders as soon as this permission came through.

The Government of India, however, refused permission and firmly stated that as a sovereign power, it could not permit the armed forces of any foreign state to pass through its boundaries. It also refuted the allegation that the Indian government had anything to do with the liberation of Dadra and Nagar Haveli and maintained that the uprising was solely a case of the local population resisting an oppressive rule.

A week later, in a gesture of protest, the Portuguese expelled Vincent Coelho, the Indian consul general in Panaji and G.A. Prabhu, the deputy consul general posted at Madgao. They were given just one day to leave Goa. In retaliation, the Indian government ordered Dr Emilo Patriko, the Portuguese consul general based in Bombay and his deputy, Dr Edvardee, to leave within forty-eight hours. After 2 August, communication between the two countries had dried up. By 15 August 1954, when the Portuguese knew there was no way they could force their way back into Dadra and Nagar Haveli, they decided to generate international pressure. They wanted to take back the lost territories and thwart any similar action supported by India in Goa, Daman and Diu. Their logic was that globalising the issue would lead to a Kashmir-like stalemate, which they could leverage to their advantage.

Their first port of call was NATO. But despite Nehru's fears, things did not go their way. NATO accepted that it was treaty-bound to help any member state whose sovereignty was under attack, but this mandate did not extend to colonies.

Left with no alternative, the Portuguese turned to the UN, of which Portugal was not even a member. It had not joined the UN precisely because it did not agree with its anti-colonial slant. Despite this, it applied for membership at the beginning of 1955 and was admitted. Ironically, India voted for its admission, unaware of the country's true intent. On 8 August 1955, Portugal filed a petition in the International Court of Justice in the Hague, for which being a member of the UN was a prerequisite. They requested the court to depute representatives from neutral countries to survey the territories under Portuguese occupation in India and report their status to the court. India initially assented to this, but both sides took opposing stands once the talks began. India wanted the Portuguese to leave the occupied territories; Portugal said no. Negotiations broke down quickly.

On 25 August, Jawaharlal Nehru strongly defended the Indian position of not permitting Portuguese forces to cross into Nagar Haveli. He stated that India was only adhering to its position of not supporting violence against local populations of the occupied territories.

Portugal then launched a diplomatic offensive in various international capitals. Though it did get some support, notably from powers with extensive colonial possessions in Africa, the USA took a contrary stand, insisting that Portugal permit greater freedom to local populations in its colonies (which in diplomatese meant it supported India).

Responding to this in the Indian Parliament, opposition parties alleged that the USA's hidden motive was to supplant Portugal in Goa and establish a military base there. Nehru denied this and assured them that under no circumstances would India permit any NATO country to have military bases in India. Whatever the reason for the USA's support, it did tilt the scales in India's favour and Portugal was isolated.

Not seeing any other way out, on 22 December 1955, Portugal converted the petition to a case in the International Court of Justice. They requested the court to advise the Government of India to permit them to send their forces into Dadra and Nagar Haveli. They claimed this was their right as these territories were an inalienable part of Portugal. The dispute dragged on for seven years and it was only after the court ruled in India's favour that the merger of Dadra and Nagar Haveli with India was officially complete. In the interim, it functioned as an independent country—the Free State of Dadra and Nagar Haveli.[255]

As the two nations sparred in the international arena, there was a lot happening in Silvassa. The celebrations of 15 August ended on a note of exhilaration and brought to an end one phase of the liberation struggle. The Azad Gomantak Dal and the RSS group readjusted their aims, preparing to retire to their camps and reassess their strategies for liberating Daman.

Wakankar, Phadke, Shantaram Vaidya and a few others left for Pune on 15 August. Bhopale, Jadhav and Purshottam Shahane, who were more closely aligned with Kajrekar, stayed behind to help him with the consolidation. Due to the ideological differences and the hot-headed elements on each side, skirmishes between them and the Goan volunteers

---

255 Joshi, p. 81.

became a regular feature. Finally, Kajrekar ordered Shahane to escort the others back to Pune.[256]

Kajrekar had been a part of the campaign from the beginning, when Phadke had first come to Lavachha to establish contact with its residents. He had stayed behind and worked as a gardener at Tapovan while plotting the fall of Dadra. He was also the one closest to Nagarwala, which is why the Goans believed that he was the one who had told Nagarwala about the theft from the treasury, a matter that they felt should have been privately resolved. Using the incident of Bhopale attacking a Goan People's Party member en route from Khanvel and the subsequent skirmishes, Lawande relieved Kajrekar of all responsibilities and asked him to leave.[257] Kajrekar eventually returned, eleven days later, after Lawande himself had been removed from his position as administrator and forced to return to the Dal camp on the border of Goa.

Lawande's fall was due to his ambition, according to some, and his dishonesty, according to others. Either way, the bone of contention was a sum of money, ₹20,000 or so, that he insisted each of the landowners of Dadra and Nagar Haveli pay the Azad Gomantak Dal. He said the money was required to raise an armed force to attack Daman in case the Portuguese managed to obtain transit rights from the Indian government. Also, with well over 1,000 soldiers in Daman, it would be easy to recapture if the Dal did not recruit and train more volunteers.

The locals felt it was impractical to attempt to capture Daman because, besides the soldiers posted there, there was

---

256 Harisinh Parmar, *Brief History of Liberation of Dadra and Nagar Haveli*, Souvenir Golden Jubilee Celebrations, 1998, p. 45.

257 Lawande, p. 249.

also the prospect of reinforcements arriving from Goa by sea. The likelihood of the Government of India permitting an armed force, even if it was the Dal's, to enter Indian territory was also minimal. Besides, when they asked Lawande for receipts for the money they gave him, he refused and stopped asking for more money. The landlords who had paid took this to be an admission of dishonesty and complained to Morarji Desai, who asked Nagarwala to remove him as administrator immediately.

On 26 August, Lawande and all the members of the Azad Gomantak Dal left Dadra and Nagar Haveli. Karmalkar, who was known for his honesty and administrative acumen, was appointed the new administrator of the liberated territories. Lawande had proposed his name to the government in Mumbai, which now played a significant role in the consolidation process, and it accepted the recommendation within a day. At the end of August, he took over the reins, and Kajrekar was appointed the chief of police.[258]

The International Court of Justice comprises a total of fifteen judges elected from among the members of the UN for a term of nine years each, with a third retiring every three years. No country is permitted to have more than one judge on the bench and two judges are co-opted temporarily from the countries that are party to the dispute. Acceptance of any judgement is voluntary, and the court has no ability to enforce its decision. A victory can only really help mobilise international opinion in favour of a country's stand.

---

258 Harisinh Parmar, *Brief History of Liberation of Dadra and Nagar Haveli*, Souvenir Golden Jubilee Celebrations, 1998, p. 43.

In their plaint, Portugal claimed that the right to passage from Daman to Nagar Haveli through Indian territory had been granted to them by a treaty signed with the Marathas under Madhav Rao II in 1779 and that the villages of Dadra and Nagar Haveli had been given to them in place of Portuguese territories captured by the Marathas north of Daman. Therefore, these were their sovereign possessions, and they had every right to defend themselves against illegal armed action that violated international law. They argued that this right had never been revoked by the British when power was transferred to them from the Marathas in 1818 or by the Indian authorities post-1947. It demanded that the right be restored and made enforceable in perpetuity.

As evidence, the Portuguese lodged the Portuguese and French translations of the original treaty, which was written in Marathi. The Indian government attempted to locate the original document, but failed. It turned out that it was in safe custody in Goa, and the Portuguese had no intention of sharing it with the Indians.

The Indian legal team led by Attorney General M.C. Setalvad,[259] assisted by the ex-attorney general of the United Kingdom, Sir Frank Soskis, and a professor of international law at Oxford, C.H.S. Waldlock, mulled various options but hit the same roadblock—the treaty's Marathi text, which was

---

259 Motilal Chimanlal Setalvad was the longest-serving Attorney General of India and held office between 1950–63. He was also the chairman of the first law commission. Since the case was lodged against the government of India demanding transit rights, he represented the government. His granddaughter Teesta Setalvad is an activist and an opponent of the current regime.

central to all their arguments against the Portuguese claim, was inaccessible![260]

The preliminary hearing of the case started on 23 September 1957 and concluded on 11 October 1957. Setalvad raised objections to the admission of the lawsuit itself. He contended that Portugal had only taken a provisional membership of the UN and the Secretary-General had not yet communicated the membership officially to India. Thus, Portugal had no right to appeal to the court. The Indian side also pointed out that the case pertained to a treaty signed before 1930 and was thus outside the jurisdiction of the court. Furthermore, Portugal had not attempted any bipartite negotiations on the issue, which was a prerequisite to hearing a case in the court. For all these reasons, the suit was inadmissible.

The hope that the case would be dismissed at an early stage was dashed when the court refused to accept the preliminary objections about jurisdiction and ruled that the issue of bipartite negotiations and the year of the treaty would be discussed as part of the suit, along with the main arguments.

In India, this decision triggered a search for the original treaty document or, at the very least, a copy of it. The Indian government entrusted the task to Dr S.M. Joshi, a noted historian and an expert on the Peshwa era. He spent time in the state government archives in the Itihas Sanshodhan Mandal (a Pune-based organisation devoted to historical research, especially Maratha history) and in the Bhandarkar Research Institute in Pune, but drew a blank. Umedsinh Paramar from Silvassa went through the Dharampur royal family archives with their permission, but also came up with nothing. Joshi found a document from 1817, signed by Balaji Bajirao Peshwa, which said that since the Portuguese had

---

260 Joshi, p. 86.

exceeded the limit for revenue collection which the Peshwa had granted to them via the treaty of 1779, the right of passage given to them through Marathi territory stood cancelled. This document, again, was of little use without the original treaty.

But Joshi's persistence paid off. He found a reference that suggested someone called Father Heras, whom he traced to St Xavier's College in Bombay, had a photograph of the original Marathi document. A search of his archives finally yielded a copy of the elusive treaty.[261]

The Indian case instantly became stronger in more ways than one.

⁓

The Free State of Dadra and Nagar Haveli, meanwhile, was evolving structures to replace the Portuguese administration. Karmalkar firmly believed that the government had to reflect the will of the people, a view strongly supported by the Morarji Desai government. In consultation with prominent citizens, he divided the region into twenty-one panchayats. The residents of each would elect a panch as their representative. The elected panchs, in turn, would elect a sarpanch and the body so constituted would be called the Varishtha Panchayat. The members of this body would work closely with the administrator in all matters pertaining to the region.

In the first-ever election held on 25 November 1954,[262] Ganpatrao Chaubal was elected sarpanch, and the Varishtha Panchayat passed a resolution asking for the state to be merged with India. Between 1954 and 1959, they passed ten more

---

261 Ibid.

262 Harisinh Parmar, *Brief History of Liberation of Dadra and Nagar Haveli*, Souvenir Golden Jubilee Celebrations, 1998, p. 87.

resolutions. The Indian government could not act on them because the case was pending before the International Court of Justice, but they used these resolutions to strengthen their legal arguments.

Through the Varishta Panchayat, the administrative machinery began fulfilling the promises Lawande had made. As a first step, the houses of the Portuguese officers with all the valuables in them were seized and auctioned off, and the money received was deposited in the treasury.

Congress Sewa Dal volunteers, under the guidance of Laljibhai Naik, spread out into the villages once more and made a complete list of tribal lands that had been usurped by the landlords. They submitted a report to the Varishtha Panchayat, which in turn, after verification, passed a resolution ordering the return of these lands to their original owners. Shamrao Patil, on behalf of the landowners, and Bhishe Guruji, a social worker trusted by the tribals, supervised the exchange of ownership.[263]

Meanwhile, in a move designed to exert pressure on the Indian government and create a communal rift, some families who had migrated to Daman sent telegrams to Nehru, at the instigation of the Portuguese, alleging that the Azad Gomantak Dal volunteers had desecrated churches. They demanded that UN observers survey the territories and submit a report. This upset Nehru, who realised that if religious polarisation occurred, it could lead to international pressure. He deputed Pinto, a Christian officer from the central intelligence services, to investigate the matter. Dr Harisinh Parmar, Solanki and other local residents escorted him around the territory and showed him that no churches had been damaged and that Christians who had stayed on were living in peace. The report

---

263 Ibid.

he subsequently wrote neutralised the Portuguese attempt to use religion as a basis for mobilising international opinion.[264]

A year after Karmalkar's appointment, the Varishtha Panchayat, while commending his honesty and sincerity, expressed dissatisfaction with his inefficient style of working and petitioned Morarji Desai for assistance. He agreed to post some retired officers of the IAS as consultants to the Panchayat. Karmalkar's successor, Dr Antonio Furtado, a Goan lawyer with nationalistic views who took over in the middle of 1954, continued in the post for five years and pioneered many reforms. During this period, the Varishtha Panchayat built schools, set up health centres, reformed the revenue collection system, and exercised the judicial function and solved disputes efficiently and transparently with the help of retired officers of the Maharashtra state, whom the administration employed on a contractual basis.

The eleventh resolution on the merger, passed in 1959, enumerated the various steps the new administration had taken in detail. In no uncertain terms, it expressed that the state had no intention of being ruled by the Portuguese who had done nothing for the ordinary person.

Despite this, the court case dragged on and a spectre of uncertainty hung over Silvassa.

The copy of the treaty that Joshi had discovered yielded some exciting information. The Portuguese had submitted their translation of the treaty in court without attaching the original, and it turned out now that the Marathi version did not have the signatures of the Portuguese representatives.

---

264 Ibid.

Also, the document ratified by Queen Maria I was merely the translation and lacked the signature of the Marathas. This meant neither document had been signed by both the parties, without which, Setalvad argued, there was no treaty.[265]

The Marathi version also proved that the Portuguese had only been granted the right to collect ₹12,000 annually as revenue. They had not been given sovereign ownership. Further, the right to revenue collection was subject to the will of the Marathas and the treaty could be rescinded at any time by the Peshwa without citing a reason. The document also stated that the right to collect revenue did not affect the ownership of the territories, which stayed with the Marathas. The words of the treaty were clear: 'Care should be taken that after the assignment [of the revenue rights] the authority of the Sarkar [the Peshwa] will meet no obstruction.'[266]

Not only that, the treaty prohibited the Portuguese from erecting any permanent structures on the land.[267] They only had 'saranjam' or revenue collection rights up to a specific amount. The Portuguese translation, however, referred to this as 'ownership'. The Indian side insisted that this mistranslation was the result of a conspiracy between the Portuguese envoy Narayan Vithal Dhume and the translator Anant Kamodi Wagh, who were close acquaintances from the same village. The document submitted by the Portuguese was thus incorrect and unreliable.

The legal team then produced a letter written by zamindars and ryots (landholders and cultivators) to the Peshwa, complaining about the unjust behaviour of the

---

265 ICJ Pleadings. Case concerning the right of passage over Indian territory (Portugal vs. India). Vol II. Rejoinder of Indian government, p. 33.
266 Ibid, p. 36.
267 Ibid, p. 47.

Portuguese. 'We approach the feet of the Master and make our representations in detail,' it said. 'Let the Master be kind enough to keep the Mahal under his direct revenue administration.'[268]

The Peshwa, in response, had written, 'The Vakil from the Firangee was always accredited to the Sarkar at Poona, and services of the Sarkar were performed by the Firangee at Goa. For this, the Mahal of Nagar Haveli, Taluka Bassein, has been granted by the Sarkar in Saranjam to the Firangee of Goa. Of late, no services to the Sarkar are rendered by the Firangee, and the Vakil does not reside in Pune. Therefore, the Mahal should be resumed.' This meant that the right to revenue collection had been terminated—and Portugal's possession of the territories was illegal.[269]

Sir Francis Soskis, the former attorney general of Britain arguing on behalf of India, quoted from a treaty dated 26 December 1878 between the British and the Portuguese. One of the clauses in it stated that the Portuguese would not use British territory to transfer arms and ammunition without its permission. He pointed out that the later treaties of 1913 and 1920 reinforced this point.

The Indian side also stated that the Dadra and Nagar Haveli insurrection was 'sudden and spontaneous' and resulted from Portuguese repression of a movement for freedom from foreign rule. It added that the insurrection was entirely carried out by 'Goans who went into Dadra and Nagar Haveli [who] were small in number and carried no arms and ammunition' and that 'the Portuguese police force withdrew from Silvassa, the administrative capital, and voluntarily entered Indian territories after being denied food and drink by the locals

---

268 Ibid, p. 142.
269 Ibid, p. 143.

for several days'. Subsequently, the people had set up their own government and were determined not to 'submit to the resubjugation by Portugal'.[270]

The Indians emphasised that there was now a 'de facto' local government in Dadra and Nagar Haveli. Their closing argument was that neither under the treaty nor as per the custom or the general principles of law was the plaint of the Portuguese sustainable.[271]

On 12 April 1960, the court, in its judgement, rejected the preliminary objections of the Indian government and accepted that the Portuguese held revenue collection rights, though not sovereign ownership. It also ruled that the Portuguese right to passage, as exercised by custom, was for the movement of private persons, civil officials and goods and did not cover armed forces, arms and ammunition. They recognised that the right to move arms and ammunition was subject to the approval of the British and, later, the Indian government.[272] India was thus well within its rights to prevent the Portuguese forces from crossing over to Dadra and Nagar Haveli.

Once the court had announced its verdict, the Indian government was free to start the process of integration. While the Portuguese, in an attempt to save face, celebrated the court's decision by claiming that their stand had been vindicated, it was a hollow victory since the judgement rendered void the possibility of sending armed forces to repossess Dadra and Nagar Haveli.

The court's decision was greeted with jubilation in Dadra and Nagar Haveli. The Varishtha Panchayat once again passed a resolution reiterating the demand for integration. This

---

270 Ibid, p. 246–247.

271 Ibid, p. 310.

272 Ibid, p. 53–54.

time, unlike the previous times, the government responded positively. H.K.L. Kapoor, an IAS officer, was sent to survey the situation on the ground. Kapoor spent considerable time in the area, speaking to the tribals, landlords, civic officials and other prominent citizens to ascertain whether the demand for a merger had popular support. Convinced that it did, he submitted a report to the Union government, based on which K.G. Badlani, also an IAS officer, was posted as the administrator to ensure the merger proceeded smoothly.

Badlani submitted a blueprint to the Union government for the administration of the territories and workforce requirements. The government sent the required personnel on loan from the Gujarat government, and the necessary administrative machinery was quickly put in place.

Badlani conducted an election in which, through a show of hands from amongst those present, twenty-one members were elected to a new Varishtha Panchayat. This body then passed a fresh resolution stating that it was the legally elected representative body of the people of Dadra and Nagar Haveli and once again requested a merger with the Union of India as per the desire of the people.

At Nehru's invitation, in August 1961, the Varishtha Panchayat members led by Badlani visited Delhi. The delegation included the sarpanch, Jayantibhai Desai, the secretary to the panchayat, Bhikubhai Pandya, and an Adivasi woman, Jammaniben Varatha, among others. Nehru met with them and assured them of immediate action in response to their demands.[273]

The following day's newspapers were full of Jammaniben Varatha. While taking leave of the prime minister, the feisty woman had invited him to her home. 'Nagar Haveli aavjo,'

---

273 *Hindustan Times*, 10 August 1961.

she said. When Nehru asked her what he would do there, she said she would cook him a nice meal of nangli (millet).

Nehru accepted the invitation, and though he did not immediately visit Nagar Haveli, he piloted the Constitution (10th Amendment) Act 1961 through the Lok Sabha, on 11 August. Presented by Lakshmi Menon, it was passed on 14 August and went to the Rajya Sabha on 16 August, where it was approved on the same day, becoming a law effective retroactively from 11 August. All that remained was the formal signing of documents, and here is where a final stumbling block arose—although an official was deputed to sign it on behalf of the Union of India, legally, there was no one to sign it on behalf of the Free State of Dadra and Nagar Haveli.

The case of Dadra and Nagar Haveli differed from all the other states that had merged with the Indian Union. In the case of the other quasi-independent states, the ruler had signed the instrument of accession or authorised someone to do so. In Hyderabad, the Indian military had overrun the state and an instrument of surrender was signed. But in the case of Dadra and Nagar Haveli, there was no single constitutional authority. The Varishtha Panchayat was, in effect, the legislature, but no one had the power to represent its collective will.

To resolve the matter, the Varishtha Panchayat of Dadra and Nagar Haveli met for the last time in Silvassa on 14 August 1961. It unanimously accepted the resignation of K.G. Badlani[274] as administrator and then elected him prime minister, authorising him to sign the instrument of accession

---

274 Badlani's one-day stint as a prime minister got him lot of recognition. However, it also gave him some trouble. When he retired, his pension was delayed by bureaucrats on the basis that there had been a break in his service by a day!

to India. On the same day, they administered him the oath of office and K.G. Badlani, IAS, found himself equivalent in protocol to Prime Minister Nehru himself as a functional head of an independent country, even if only for a single day.

On 16 August 1961, in the presence of all the panchayat members, Badlani heard his name being called out and rose to complete the task he had been assigned. With the signing of the merger, the people of Dadra and Nagar Haveli became Indian citizens with immediate effect. The process of the emancipation of Goa, Daman and Diu also set into motion. On December 1961, Indian forces entered the three remaining Portuguese-owned territories in India and liberated them from foreign rule.

Although the volunteers who fought for the liberation of Dadra and Nagar Haveli did not directly contribute to this last phase of the liberation struggle, there can be no doubt that it was their courageous initiative and persistence that resulted in the formation of the Republic of India as we know it today.

Curfew Clamped On All Goa Towns

'FIGHTING' IN PROGRESS AT SELVASA

KARWAR, Aug. 1.

NIGHT curfew has been clamped down on all important towns in the Portuguese settlement of Goa, according to passengers arriving here from Goa. Strong military guards were patrolling the frontiers, they said.

The passengers added they saw Negro soldiers digging trenches on both the flanks of the Paingini bridge, on the chief road link between Karwar and Goa, about six miles from the border.

Reliable reports reaching Vapi today from Selvasa. seat of the administration of the Portuguese enclave of Nagar Haveli, said the town had not yet been fully " liberated."

The reports indicated that " fighting " was in progress right inside the town between volunteers of the Azad Gomantak Dal and Portuguese police.

These volunteers had this morning " occupied " Piparia. The volunteers had captured large quantities of arms and ammunition from Portuguese police during their march on the town.

Meanwhile, the Goan People's Party volunteers with a large number of Warlis were marching on Selvasa from the neighbouring Lahori village which they liberated on Saturday.

FOUR VILLAGES FREED

A G.P.P. leader in an interview said if they reached Selvasa in time they would give all possible help to the Gomantak Dal volunteers to " liberate " the town.

The Warlis have on their way freed four more unnamed villages.

The torrential rains and the swollen rivers have made all approaches to Selvasa difficult.

Mrs Godavari Parulekar, Leftist Warli leader, who is guiding the G.P.P. " liberation " movement. said according to information

Continued on back page col. 6

Newspaper clipping from the *Hindustan Times* reporting on a curfew imposed in Silvassa due to unrest, published on 1 August 1954

Hindusthan Standard

ISSUED SIMULTANEOUSLY FROM DELHI AND CALCUTTA

291   DELHI, Monday 2 August 1954

Selvasa On Verge Of Falling

Fighting Raging In Heart Of Town

VAPI, AUG. 1.—Reliable reports reaching Vapi today from Selvasa, seat of administration of the Portuguese enclave of Nagar Haveli, said that the town has not yet been fully "liberated". The reports indicated that "fighting" was in progress right inside the town between the volunteers of the Azad Gomantak Dal and the Portuguese police.

These volunteers had this morning "occupied" Piparia, a village on the outskirts of Selvasa.

The volunteers had captured large quantities of arms and ammunition from the Portuguese police during their march on the town.

Meanwhile, the Goan Peoples Party volunteers with a large number of Warlis were marching on Selvasa from the neighbouring Lahodi village which they liberated on Saturday.

A G.P.P. leader said that if they reach Selvasa on time they would give all possible help to the Gomantak Dal volunteers to "liberate" the town.

The Warlis have on their way

Continued On Page 5, Col. 4

Fighting Raging In Selvasa

Continued from page 1, Col. 7
freed four more unnamed villages.

Torrential rains and the swollen rivers have made all approaches to Selvasa difficult.

Sm. Godavari Parulekar, the Leftist Warli leader, who is guiding the G.P.P. "liberation" movement said according to information reaching her in Udwa, the Warlis and the volunteers were meeting with limited resistance.

AIM OF LIBERATION

Sm. Parulekar, who is now camping in Udwa, said according to her plans the volunteers and the Warlis were to "liberate" the entire south half of Nagar Haveli enclave before launching a "mass attack" on Selvasa. This attack was scheduled for Tuesday next.

"It is quite possible that the movement gained tempo and the volunteers were able to capture Selvasa ahead of schedule," she said commenting on reports of the fall of the town to liberation forces.

The main objective of the Warlis in "liberation" of the Portuguese territories was to end "slave labour that is prevalent there", Sm. Parulekar said.

She had told the volunteers that immediately on "liberation" the administration of the villages should be passed on to the village panchayats and the volunteers should not attempt at land distribution or rent adjustments, she added.—P.T.I.

11 Policemen Arrested

SURAT, AUGUST 1.—Eleven Portuguese policemen of Damaun who had crossed over to Indian territory in "plain clothes" were taken into custody by Indian police today.

The arrested persons have been brought to Vapi.—P.T.I.

नगरहवेली मुक्त होणार असल्याबद्दल दि. २ ऑगस्ट १९५४ रोजीच्याच वृत्तपत्रात आलेली माहिती.

Newspaper clipping from the *Hindusthan Standard* reporting on the fighting in progress in Silvassa, 2 August 1954

SELVASA LIBERATED BY VOLUNTEERS

PORTUGUESE OFFICERS ESCAPE WITH MONEY AND ARMS

VAPI, Aug. 2.

SELVASA, the administrative headquarters of the Portuguese enclave of Nagar Haveli, was liberated today.

The Indian Tricolour was hoisted over the office of the Administrator and the police station at midday.

All resistance was reported to have ended this morning and when about 100 volunteers of the Azad Gomantak Dal marched into Selvasa from three sides at 9-30 a.m. they found that the three Portuguese officers in the town had fled. The volunteers then peacefully occupied the police station and the magistrate's court within half an hour.

The town was calm this afternoon. Its 5,000 inhabitants offered the Dal volunteers their full co-operation. The Dal then called a conference of village patels with a view to setting up a new administration in the area.

The three Portuguese officers, Capt. Fidelgo, Administrator; Capt. Pageto, the police chief; and Mr Falcao, magistrate, who fled, are understood to have carried with them arms and ammunition and Rs 1,80,000 from the treasury which the liberation volunteers found empty on occupation.

The Dal volunteers set free two women whom the Portuguese had detained yesterday.

With the liberation of Selvasa nearly a third of the 42,000 population of Nagar Haveli enclave has been freed from Portuguese domination.—P.T.I.

Newspaper clipping from the *Hindustan Times* reporting on the liberation of Silvassa, published 2 August 1954

Triumphant volunteers gathered together after the liberation of
Silvassa, August 1954

Volunteers celebrating with locals in the aftermath of the struggle,
August 1954

Entrance to the Dadra police post

Entrance to the Udhawa police post where Fidaldo and his men
surrendered on 11 August 1954

Freedom fighters gathered outside the office of the chief of police in
Silvassa to mark twenty-five years of independence, 1979

Postscript

IN Salman Rushdie's words, 'Books choose their authors; the act of creation is not necessarily a rational or conscious one.'

I do not know if this is always true, but it certainly rings true for this book. I did not go looking for the story—it came looking for me. Once it entered my life, it latched on to me so fiercely that I knew I would never be at peace till I wrote it. I learned about the satyagraha launched against the Portuguese in Goa because my grandfather had participated in it, but an armed struggle? I knew little about it until I met the Manolkars on a train.

At the beginning of 2020, my wife Sarita and I were on a train to Nasik, hoping to gather material for *In the Footsteps of Rama: Travels with the Ramayana*. Seated opposite us was an elderly gentleman and his middle-aged son. Hearing them speak Marathi, I introduced myself and we got talking. The father–son duo, Arvind and Mayuresh Manolkar, were heading to Gwalior from Delhi. When I asked Mayuresh what they were in Delhi for, he told me that his father was a freedom fighter and that they had gone to meet the home minister. Mayuresh proudly added that his father had been part of the only successful people-led armed struggle during the Indian freedom movement. I didn't know what to make of the statement and upon seeing the lack of understanding on my face (something they were probably entirely used to!), he told me about this battle. Listening to it was so inspiring that I knew it had to be taken to a larger audience.

I got caught up in finishing my book and later, promoting it, and then moved on to other projects. The story, however, did not loosen its grip on me, and I kept chasing the Manolkars for more details. Finally, after almost a year, on one of their periodic visits to Delhi, they met me and handed over an issue of a souvenir with a detailed description of the struggle. That's where I first read about the participation of Lata Mangeshkar, Mohammad Rafi, Sudhir Phadke and Babasaheb Purandare.

As I read and reread the article, I noticed many gaps in the narrative. It did not, for instance, mention anything about the planning and coordination that went into the resistance, nor where and how the arms were procured or about the role of the Azad Gomantak Dal, which was mentioned only in passing. Arvind-ji readily admitted that he knew very little about these aspects because he had entered the battle after the capture of Naroli and left after Silvassa fell. By now, most of the dramatis personae had passed on, and the ones I was blessed to meet knew only as much as Arvind-ji did. I faced a blank wall.

Then, my cousin Milind got me an audience with the noted historian Babasaheb Purandare. He was almost ninety-nine when I met him, and he promised to talk to me if I returned after a few days since his calendar was packed for the month. But before the meeting could take place, he passed on too. All I got from our meeting was that arms had been procured from Hyderabad, and Mohd Wahab had taken them to a tree near Golconda Fort for this.

Based on this information, I landed at Golconda Fort and asked around if anyone knew where Mohd Wahab lived. Coincidentally, the second person I asked was his son, Mohd Javed, now a tourist guide, who immediately took me to the baobab tree, the hiding place of the arms. One more part of the puzzle fell into place. The rest of the Hyderabad story was easy to piece together.

The information that I now possessed included details of the operation from the point of view of the volunteers from Pune. I knew nothing about the Azad Gomantak Dal and its leaders, though the name of Prabhakar Sinari popped up a few times in the documents I had accessed. I knew practically no one in Goa, and looking for someone by a name in a large state was worse than looking for a needle in a thousand haystacks. As I mulled over this challenge, a Facebook post by Diana Charles, an Orkut-era friend I had not met for a while, caught my attention. She had posted something about the liberation of Goa, and I messaged her to ask her if she knew any freedom fighters from there. When I explained the context to her, she replied that she did not know anyone directly, as she had since settled in Mumbai, but she promised to circulate the message to all her Goa groups. She did, and within two days, I got five contacts, and one of them sent me a list of telephone numbers, of which one was of Sinari himself! He was alive and in good health and had written a book about his contribution to the cause. I called him, but was told he had done his duty towards his country and saw no reason to discuss it. After some persuasion, he relented, invited me home, and told me his side of the story. From there, the link to Lawande and the others was easy to follow.

From the same network, I obtained the number of Prabhakar Vaidya's daughter but could not contact her as she was travelling in remote areas where the connectivity was very poor. I kept trying, and when I did manage to connect, it turned out that she was due to visit Delhi soon and would be staying at a hotel near my house. We met the very next day and she gave me a copy of Vaidya's memoirs, which gave me insights into events after the fall of Silvassa, and probably the only complete description of the battle of Khanvel.

It remained for me to visit the places I had been reading about, so I took off to Silvassa for a week. I just had a telephone number (given by Mayuresh Manolkar) for Deepak Jadhav, a former president of the BJP unit of Dadra and Nagar Haveli. Mayuresh did not know it yet, but he had put me in touch with a person who was keen to bring out all the different aspects of the liberation story, including the role of the tribal population of Dadra and Nagar Haveli in it. Deepak Bhai cancelled all engagements and spent the next seven days taking us to the homes of the various freedom fighters, who told us their stories. He also took us deep into the jungles and introduced us to several tribals who had participated in the struggle. People in their eighties or early nineties spoke about the day they had got together to throw out the fanaga. The name of Jatruben Vansabhai Ghoom came up repeatedly. When I asked Deepak Bhai, he took me to Ghoom's home, where her sons now lived.

While I was with them, and some others whom her sons had summoned, having everything translated from their dialect into Hindi, a young lady walked into the courtyard where we were gathered and overheard us. 'You want to know about Grandma?' she asked. Ghoom's granddaughter, an engineer working with Infosys in Bengaluru, was home on vacation. She sat down and told me the whole story about her grandmother's role in the struggle.

As more and more layers of the magnificent story unravelled, I became increasingly obsessed with it. I started looking for written material, but found that besides disjointed accounts by those who had participated in it, and a few newspaper reports, there was nothing in the public realm. That's when it transformed from an idea into a mission—I knew I had to write the book so that every Indian would know about the courage, fortitude, integrity and selfless love exhibited by these magnificent people.

When I met the surviving participants, I found that not of them wanted any accolades for the work they had done. Today, when we survive on artificial likes and friends in the virtual world, these men stood out for me as real heroes—people who did the right thing and then returned to their simple, everyday lives.

This a real story about real heroism that I chanced to uncover. Since nothing happens purely by chance, it's evident to me that the story chose me and I owe it a debt of gratitude that I must repay. Now that you have read it, do tell me if my telling of it has been worthy of the faith the story reposed in me.

I await your comments on my social media handles—@ neeleshkulkarnii on Instagram and Neelesh Kulkarni on LinkedIn and Facebook.